Lincoln Christian College

D1309671

Joseph Smith's
NEW ENGLAND HERITAGE

Joseph Smith's NEW ENGLAND HERITAGE

Influences of Grandfathers
Solomon Mack and Asael Smith

by

RICHARD LLOYD ANDERSON

Published By
Deseret Book Company
Salt Lake City, Utah
1971

JSEPH SMITH, JR.

Copyright 1971
by
Deseret Book Company
Library of Congress Catalog Card No. 74-186263
ISBN 87747-460-5

TO MY WIFE, CARMA ROSE DE JONG

From New England school days until now,
she has never questioned the value of my research.

Baker & Taylor

4/70

15 May '74

50243

Contents

Illustrations

Notes on Illustrations (p. 221) contains credits and background on pictures.

Preface

One who understands the moral power of the individuals surrounding Joseph Smith will never see him in quite the same way again. Asael Smith wrote to his children in the hope that his good qualities would "revive and live in you," a process at work to some extent in every family. Since Joseph Smith's grandparents largely created the influences of his youth, the formation of the boy is perceived through his family background. Research transforms empty names into vital people, and isolated facts into gripping biographies. Asael Smith and Solomon Mack were part of the dynamic era that founded a great nation, but their moral fiber contributed to the later founding of an important church. Although their venturesome lives are fascinating by themselves, they also bear upon a most significant issue.

Since Joseph Smith claimed modern direct revelation, his reliability is the central historical question. No approach throws more light on his early life than close study of his environment. Careful biography of the Prophet begins with an accurate understanding of the operating convictions of his home, and these stemmed from his grandparents. Sweeping statements about the general religious attitude in early nineteenth-century America will not do—even studying early New England or Vermont is not enough. No one really knows Joseph Smith's background until he knows which influences of that time and region were operative in his family. So nothing less than detailed portraits of his immediate ancestors can furnish answers. And these must throw intense light on their personalities. That is why the writings of each grandfather are published here with their life stories. Nothing reveals personality as effectively as self-expression.

Joseph Smith's common image is badly distorted, since reputable publishers continue to print astonishing misinformation from pseudo-experts on Mormonism and its founder. But serious researchers distrust Joseph Smith's biographies of current national reputation. This founder of a modern revealed religion may always be controversial, but that is no excuse for canonizing imaginative literature as history. In this situation, everyone has to take firsthand evidence and judge for himself—a practical solution, for no religion surpasses Mormonism in the preservation of the authentic documents of its early years. In fact, the last decade marks a new age in classification and duplication of library materials, to say nothing of the availability of papers in private hands. This means that historical material on Joseph Smith has at least doubled in recent years, making possible a fairly objective agreement on the main sources for each period of his life. This book begins a series on the Mormon Prophet, narrating a leading phase of his life from all reliable records and including the essential documents on which interpretation must be based. Evidence about Mormonism will speak for itself.

Acknowledgments

Thanks must be expressed to those that have co-operated in making these materials available: to Brigham Young University for time and research grants; to Brigham Young University librarians, including Adele Manwaring for her efficiency in procuring missing publications through interlibrary loans; to LDS Church President Joseph Fielding Smith and Church Historian Howard W. Hunter for permission to publish many sources, including the facsimile of Asael Smith's family address; to Assistant Church Historian Earl E. Olson and his staff—particularly archivist Dean Jessee for endless patience with requests and inquiries; to the LDS Genealogical Society staff for their helpfulness in utilizing their magnificent source collection—and to Robert J. Tarte, Boston Branch librarian; to friends who have been generous in consultation, particularly Professors Richard L. Bushman of Boston University, Milton V. Backman, Jr., and Russell Rich of Brigham Young University, and Donald Q. Cannon of the University of Maine, Portland; to Archibald Hanna and Yale University for library assistance and permission to publish George A. Smith's correspondence; to Mrs. Charles Potter and Essex Institute for assistance and permission to publish Asael Smith's 1796 letter in facsimile; to Mrs. Kristin Bowman and Misses Sandra Compton and Pamela Flynn, my secretaries, who checked research leads, filed, and typed; to Robert Yukes and Miss Nancy Richards, who each took personal time to locate and gather materials from Massachusetts archives; to David H. Horne, president of the Asael Smith Descendants, for his courteous support and willingness to share Asael Smith's Bible, in his possession. Finally, production details open new problems to writers. William

James Mortimer, manager of Deseret Book Company, has cordially solved difficult problems, and editor (and personal friend) Gary Gillespie has gone many extra miles in making the printing as perfect as possible. All who have helped produce a book of serious research can never be named—some additional recognitions are found in the notes.

Source Note

Behind Joseph Smith's vigorous grandparents are equally interesting sources from which their lives were reconstructed. Thus Notes on Text (p. 161) are the foundation of this study. For that reason they have been set in easily readable type. Facts and relationships appear there that could not readily fit into the biographical narratives.

The footprints of the Smiths and Macks are in public records in a dozen major localities in New England, but their personalities live in their writings. Their manuscripts are preferred sources, necessitating some general observations on their treatment here. Most of the unpublished Smith and Mack documents are carefully preserved in the archives of the Church Historian's Office in Salt Lake City. Important manuscripts elsewhere have their location identified.

These documents have been reproduced here by scholarly methods, but for an audience not restricted to scholars. A researcher with a manuscript and a reader of a book do not have identical goals. Therefore, spelling errors are not published, modernized spelling is used in certain regular cases, and punctuation and capitalization have been frequently adjusted in quotations. Slavish literalism in this regard may be an abdication of the historian's main duty—to aid his documents to communicate with his reader. Despite some negative comment, Solomon Mack does not spell badly. Like much writing from his time, his prose needs slight editing for good readability. If this makes Asael or John Smith spell a bit better than they really did, perhaps the distortion is insignificant. Asael was an experienced town clerk and wrote better than average for his day. However, care has been taken to reproduce exact wording of all documents quoted. Additions or substitutions appear in brackets, and words subtracted are replaced by the standard ellipsis sign. Solomon Mack's *Narrative* (chapter 3) preserves original paging in brackets so that citations may easily be identified.

The writings of Asael Smith and Solomon Mack are reprinted in this book, with many unpublished comments from Lucy Mack Smith on the early history of both families. Serious writers revise their first drafts, and both Solomon Mack and his daughter Lucy did the same. The published versions sluffed off many interesting details as trivial; yet such matters are vital to biographers. But Lucy's first draft of her family story is almost completely preserved, mostly in her own handwriting. This is a tremendous fact, and adds to what has been known about Martha Coray, the secretary for Lucy Mack Smith (discussed in my "Circumstantial Confirmation of the First Vision Through Reminiscences," *Brigham Young University Studies,* vol. 9 [1969], pp. 386-88). Lucy's first version proves that editors Martha and Howard Coray preserved her record faithfully, for their finished product incorporates her handwritten recollections with very few basic modifications. On the other hand, Lucy Smith clearly intended to supplement her first draft, for her manuscript has numerous additions in her hand and a few in the reviser's hand. A few parts of the published Lucy Smith record are not found in her own manuscript; however, she was responsible for these additions, for she gave Orson Pratt written permission to publish "all those manuscripts you have, once belonging to me" (Letter of Feb. 4, 1854, Nauvoo, Ill., cit. Kate B. Carter [ed.], *Our Pioneer Heritage,* vol. 3 [Salt Lake City, 1960], p. 125). Thus Orson Pratt's publication in 1853 was Lucy's revised work, and one must designate her handwritten narrative as a "preliminary manuscript," the name it carries in footnote citations herein.

Later editions of Lucy Mack Smith have made some textual modifications, so this study has utilized her initial printing of 1853. Consequently, page numbers herein correspond to *Biographical Sketches of Joseph Smith*, the 1853 edition, conveniently reprinted by Arno Press and the New York Times in 1969. Undoubtedly the most popular version is that edited by Preston Nibley as the *History of Joseph Smith by His Mother*. Page numbers of this can generally be found by the context of a given quotation. Orson Pratt's full title of Lucy Smith's history included biography of both Joseph Smith "and his progenitors for many generations." That is precisely what Lucy's introduction to her preliminary manuscript contemplated. She reflected upon her unique knowledge: "none on earth do know as fully as myself, the entire history of those of whom I speak and all those intimately connected with them." Furthermore, Joseph Smith's mother saw him in the context of a religious inheritance, for she wished to trace not only the lives of the Prophet and his parents, "but likewise to give a sketch of their progenitors and the dealing of God with them also."

Why is it this babbler gains so many followers and retains them? Because I possess the principle of love. All I can offer the world [is] a good heart and a good hand.

Mormons can testify whether I am willing to lay down my life for a Mormon. If it has been demonstrated that I have been willing to die for a Mormon, I am bold to declare before heaven that I am just as ready to die for a Presbyterian, a Baptist, or any other denomination.

It is a love of liberty which inspires my soul. Civil and religious liberty was diffused into my soul by my grandfathers while they dandled me on their knees. And shall I want friends? No.

JOSEPH SMITH, JR.
Journal kept by Willard Richards
July 9, 1843

Prologue

Character assassination predates history, but responsible historians attempt to set the record straight. Joseph Smith published his life story to counteract false reports, to present "the facts as they have transpired in relation both to myself and the Church."[1] He had invited controversy by claiming that God called him as a prophet to criticize and correct a withered Christianity. His first visions came in his youth; hence the importance of understanding his family environment. An objective and intimate picture is possible of the influences upon young Joseph Smith. More is known than ever before of the parents and grandparents that fashioned the ideals of his home. Later in life Joseph Smith spoke of "love of liberty" (certainly one of his dominant characteristics) that was "diffused into my soul by my grandfathers while they dandled me on their knees."[2] In their homes were molded the personalities of Joseph Smith, Sr., and his wife, Lucy Mack Smith, parents and creators of the Prophet's immediate environment.

The books debunking Joseph Smith typically begin by downgrading his immediate ancestors. We read that his "was a crude and credulous line." Even the biography still mislabeled as definitive echoes this opinion in more sophisticated prose. Joseph Smith's father was "avowedly Christian but basically irreligious"; the mother's father finally came to "senile mysticism." These judgments are enormous exaggerations, with intended implications for Joseph Smith's life. But his grandparents deserve to stand on their own merits. Their lives are here studied in detail from their own writings, enriched

CHAPTER 1

Prologue

Character assassination predates history, but responsible historians attempt to set the record straight. Joseph Smith published his life story to counteract false reports, to present "the facts as they have transpired in relation both to myself and the Church."[1] He had invited controversy by claiming that God called him as a prophet to criticize and correct a withered Christianity. His first visions came in his youth; hence the importance of understanding his family environment. An objective and intimate picture is possible of the influences upon young Joseph Smith. More is known than ever before of the parents and grandparents that fashioned the ideals of his home. Later in life Joseph Smith spoke of "love of liberty" (certainly one of his dominant characteristics) that was "diffused into my soul by my grandfathers while they dandled me on their knees."[2] In their homes were molded the personalities of Joseph Smith, Sr., and his wife, Lucy Mack Smith, parents and creators of the Prophet's immediate environment.

The books debunking Joseph Smith typically begin by downgrading his immediate ancestors. We read that his "was a crude and credulous line." Even the biography still mislabeled as definitive echoes this opinion in more sophisticated prose. Joseph Smith's father's father was "avowedly Christian but basically irreligious"; the mother's father finally came to "senile mysticism." These judgments are enormous exaggerations, with intended implications for Joseph Smith's life. But his grandparents deserve to stand on their own merits. Their lives are here studied in detail from their own writings, enriched

by early family histories, letters, and recollections, sup-
plemented by town and church minutes, and checked
against deeds, wills, censuses, and assessment lists. A
story of responsibility and moral heroism emerges that
matches the personal philosophy that both grandfathers
candidly expressed. If they did not achieve national fame,
they at least represented the solid virtues that founded
their nation. Their moral excellence was Joseph Smith's
heritage.

The books sympathetic to Joseph Smith typically call
the roll of illustrious forbears, perhaps with an unstated
premise that outstanding ancestors have outstanding
descendants. Yet physiological inheritance is neither
evaluated nor dealt with here. However, the main en-
vironmental forces about the Mormon Prophet can be
clearly identified. Value structures are formed by con-
scious and unconscious reaction to personalities clustered
around the impressionable individual. Joseph Smith's
warm love for his parents and their positive affection
for their parents are historical realities. Joseph Smith
was deeply influenced by his older brothers and even
more by his parents. Through them the ideals of his
grandparents were effectively transmitted to the young
man who claimed visions. Any other view badly underes-
timates the powers of obedience and imitation that
characterize his family.

The riddle of Joseph Smith exists partly because
malicious detractors slandered the rising Prophet. It
could hardly be otherwise in a static, rural society that
aggressively resisted change. In Joseph Smith's own words,
the moment his revelations were known, "rumor with
her thousand tongues was all the time employed in cir-
culating tales about my father's family, and about myself." Such distortion demands knowledge of what went
on within his family. Outside sources cannot really
solve this problem, for those with the inside story are
insiders. In other words, statements of spiteful neighbors

are beside the point when the Smith family itself is available for study. Far too many biographers have believed accusations without really investigating their basis. That cannot be done without entering the Smith household and understanding its motives and manners. Joseph Smith was still a young man, heavily under his family's influence, when he announced his early visions. If the grandparents are only part of the picture, they are nevertheless a very significant part. Their profiles outline the characteristics that came to Joseph Smith through his parents. The convictions and attitudes of these grandparents go far in portraying the true personality of their grandson.

MATERNAL LINE OF JOSEPH SMITH, 1805-1844

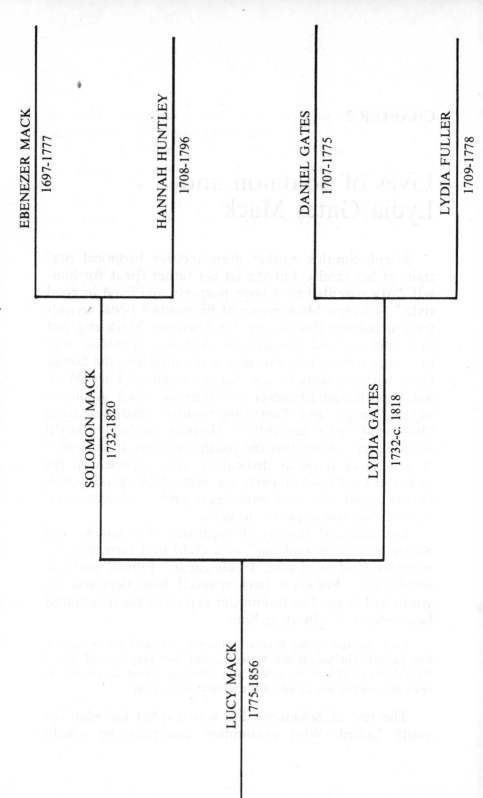

EBENEZER MACK
1697-1777

HANNAH HUNTLEY
1708-1796

DANIEL GATES
1707-1775

LYDIA FULLER
1709-1778

SOLOMON MACK
1732-1820

LYDIA GATES
1732-c. 1818

LUCY MACK
1775-1856

CHAPTER 2

Lives of Solomon and Lydia Gates Mack

Joseph Smith's mother drew incisive historical portraits of her family, but she let her father speak for himself. "My parents had a large property and lived in good
style," Solomon Mack wrote of his youth.[3] Local records
tend to confirm this picture, for Ebenezer Mack engaged
in numerous land transactions. Although a middle son,
his father named him executor and willed him the family
farm, with the duty to care for his mother.[4] Lucy Mack
Smith portrayed Ebenezer and Hannah Mack as direct-
ing a "happy and flourishing family" and displaying
"habits of strict morality."[5] Hannah probably taught
school later, "instructing the youth for about thirty years."
A woman of religious dedication, she "experienced the
power of God from an early age, with all the good morals
of life," and she died with great faith, "rejoicing and
wishing her last moments to come."[6]

But financial tragedy disorganized this family, and
Solomon was "bound out" as a child to a farmer in his
neighborhood of Lyme, Connecticut.[7] Forced early to
self-reliance, Solomon later realized how deprived his
youth had been. The taskmaster exploited the indentured
boy instead of educating him:

> I was treated by my master as his property and not as his fel-
> low mortal. He taught me to work, and was very careful that I
> should have little or no rest. From labor he never taught me to
> read or spoke to me at all on the subject of religion.[8]

The rest of Solomon's life was a quest for what his
youth lacked. With uncommon enterprise he sought

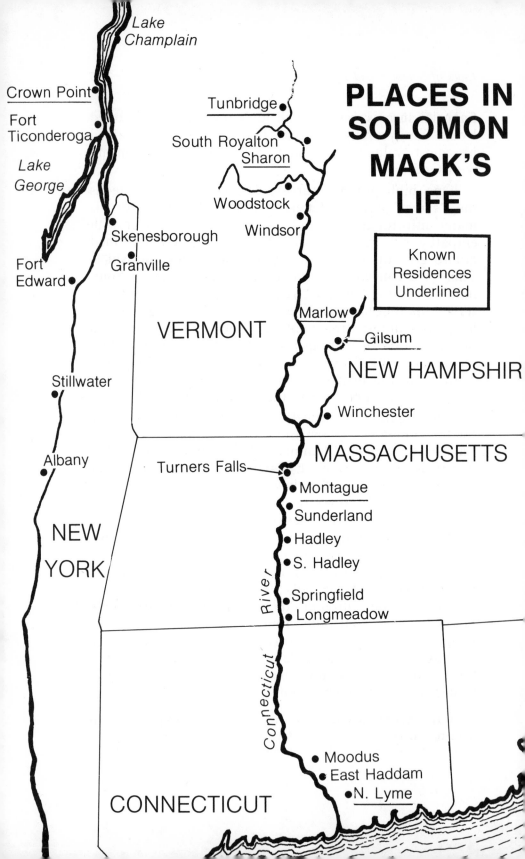

financial success, but through life's reverses was haunted by his family's religious conviction. In the end he gained his most valued possession, a satisfying relationship with God.

One bibliographer surveys Solomon Mack's life as the "career of an unlettered New Englander with his many unfortunate ups and downs."[9] A biographer with empathy will rather stress the heroism of one determined not to give up in the face of overwhelming hardships. There is a constant tone of responsible morality in Solomon's writings. Though "frequently abused," he steadily served his time until of age. In later life he still resented his early unfair treatment, but nevertheless declined the retaliation of naming his master. Solomon gave him credit for being "very kind to me," providing help and comfort in a critical sickness, though surmising his possible motive as preserving an able worker's life.[10]

On attaining his freedom, Solomon Mack enlisted for the campaigns of the French and Indian War in the Lake George-Lake Champlain sector. Exposing his life to bullets and fevers, he displayed marked bravery under danger and concern for those about him. "In the year 1755," Solomon reports of his early twenties, "I enlisted under Captain Harris and went to Fort Edward"—and the enlistment rolls verify every fact named.[11] Two years later he "mustered two teams in the King's service," freighting supplies to the front at Fort Edward.[12] Because his oxen were lost, he took a companion to search their previous route through dangerous forest. Suddenly Solomon Mack confronted four hostile Indians some 150 yards ahead, armed with knives, tomahawks, and guns. With just nerve plus a single reinforcement 100 yards behind, Solomon "saw no other way to save myself only to deceive them by stratagem":

I exclaimed like this: "Rush on! Rush on! Brave boys, we'll have the devils! We'll have the devils!" I had no other weapon only a staff. But I ran towards them, and the other man appearing in sight, gave them a terrible fright, and I saw them no more. But I am bound to say the grass did not grow under my feet.[13]

In this case, history repeated itself, as this bold strategy was later used by his prophet-grandson. The operating tradition of this family was to squarely face its problems. When Joseph Smith first received the ancient plates, neighborhood gangs formed to steal them. Lucy Mack Smith relates her son's intuitive apprehension before one such attempt, prompting him to secure the record under the hearthstones:

> This was done as speedily as possible, but the hearth was scarcely relaid when a large company of men well-armed came rushing up to the house. Joseph threw open the doors, and taking a hint from the stratagem of his grandfather Mack, halooed as if he had a legion at hand, in the meanwhile giving the word of command with great emphasis; while all the male portion of the family, from the father down to little Carlos, ran out of the house with such fury on the mob that it struck them with terror and dismay. And they fled before the little Spartan band into the woods, where they dispersed themselves to their several homes.[14]

Solomon Mack's daring was unselfish. During French and Indian War service he marched with thousands in the bloody and useless frontal assault on Fort Ticonderoga. Here he did not hang back, but "marched to the breastworks,"[15] where hundreds were killed attempting to storm a fortified wall of logs stacked eight feet high.[16] The waves of assaulting troops were met with a deadly, "damnable fire."[17] Historians can make war statistical— for Solomon it was personal: "I escaped very narrowly by a musket ball passing under my chin, perhaps within half an inch of my neck."[18] He shared the reluctant retreat of the English-American forces, impatient at incompetent leadership. Tactics now became defensive, and Solomon was sent on massive patrol with the forces of Rogers and Putnam to cut off French-Indian parties that had ambushed a supply train. But this Colonial force itself was ambushed, and Solomon Mack faced the ultimate test, which he impressively passed. His unit led a long formation strung out the better part of a mile in single file. First was his commanding officer, Major Israel Putnam, who was captured in the first attack, though he miraculously survived savage treatment. Solomon Mack's own story is a glittering bit of this mosaic: "The enemy rose like a cloud and fired a volley upon us. . . . [T]he tomahawks and bullets [were] flying around my ears like hailstones."[19] A ranger also remembered the "severe fire," accompanied by "the hideous war-whoop of the Indians, and we found ourselves nearly surrounded."[20] Safety lay in immediate retreat and regrouping. Running at full force, Solomon cleared a huge obstacle:

> And as I ran I looked [a] little one side, where I saw a man wounded (the Indians close to him), who immediately with my help got into the circle.[21]

Solomon Mack successfully gambled his own life for that of another. His unit repulsed the attack, then gradually drove their opponents, from the field. Major Rogers praised the actions of Mack's Connecticut volunteers. Although "considerably disordered" by the first assault, they "afterwards rallied and did good service"; all fought with a "vigor and resolution" that broke the surprise attack of incomparable native warriors.[22] Solomon Mack impressively shared this achievement in bravery.[23]

The energy of Solomon Mack was exceptional. Before later military service in the Revolution, he was a merchant, land developer, shipmaster, mill operator, and farmer. Though a fateful series of reverses canceled profits, his initiative poured out. Even Solomon's wedding is part of this picture, for he married well in 1759, "shortly after becoming acquainted" with Lydia Gates, daughter of a prominent Connecticut deacon. Solomon next sold goods to the army at Crown Point, on Lake Champlain, for some two years, but his lack of education prevented good accounting, with the loss of "what I had accumulated by hard industry for several years."[24] Army service had earned "a handsome sum of silver and gold," which he invested in 1,600 acres of wilderness in northern New York, only to lose it after badly gashing his leg, which prevented performing contractual obligations to clear homestead lots and build cabins.[25] This period saw the sea venture of carrying cargo from a New England port to New York City—but high profits were destroyed on return by shipwreck off Long Island.[26]

Deeds in several localities indicate Solomon's farming at this time. "I went to Lyme and purchased a farm," Solomon says of his first soldier's earnings. This was after "the biggest part of the summer" of 1756, and land records precisely support his narrative.[27] Eight acres were added after the campaign of 1758, with more expansion in 1759 (the year of his marriage), and further acreages in 1761. But "Solomon Mack of Lyme" (as he is named on Connecticut deeds) closed out these holdings between 1762 and 1766, disposing of 127 acres with houses and farm buildings.[28] In the meantime he joined several relatives to pioneer new land in southern New Hampshire. He moved some 130 miles north to Marlow in 1761 and remained over ten years. This was a primitive life: "When we moved there it was no other than a desolate and dreary wilderness. Only four families resided within forty miles."[29] Solomon's title to 100 acres matured in 1767, and that year he was elected game warden, the office of "deer reeve."[30] His deed for an additional seventy-six acres in 1770 mentioned "said Mack's old house," indicating improvements and construction of a better dwelling.[31] His toil is symbolized by the 1773 conveyance by "Solomon Mack of Marlow" of fifty acres "where the labor is done," no doubt the previous clearing of heavy forest.[32] Solomon next moved to nearby Gilsum, New Hampshire, where the deeds name "a sawmill and grist mill" owned by Elisha Mack. Responsible family tradi-

SITE OF ELISHA AND SOLOMON MACK'S MILLS, GILSUM, NEW HAMPSHIRE

tion associated Elisha "with his brother Solomon" in building "the first mills and the first bridge" in Gilsum. Solomon's mention of the sawmill (and his encounter with its waterwheel) confirms this vocation there.[33]

Solomon, Jr., and the mother of the Prophet were born at Gilsum in 1773 and 1775. Lucy was a child of the Revolution, for the battles of Lexington and Concord had been fought that spring. She was the last of eight children, but her father contributed energetically to the establishment of his country. Early war years saw a critical lack of gunpowder in the Colonies. Washington wrote of the "gloomy prospect" of shortage in 1775: "our want of powder is inconceivable." When state legislatures encouraged local production of the nitrate saltpeter and development of powder mills, Solomon was at the center of activity. He traveled to his brother-in-law's in his native Connecticut to learn how to manufacture saltpeter; then he visited Springfield and Longmeadow, in western Massachusetts, to build this technology there. He was then "sent for from town to town" at wages of "one dollar per day."[34] But war-related contributions were not enough for Solomon, who next was in active military affairs:

I then enlisted into the American army. I soon mustered two teams and carried baggage to Skenesborough. I afterwards enlisted into a company of artillery for a short campaign.[35]

This did not end his Revolutionary service, but a severe accident about 1777 demands comment. Recuperating from sickness, Solomon visited his son, who was felling trees:

[A] tree fell on me and crushed me almost all to pieces—beat the breath out of my body. My son took me up for dead. I, however, soon recovered, but have not to this day recovered the use of my limbs, which was 34 years ago.[36]

Further agonies were in store. "Soon recovered" translates to two months immovable on his back, followed by bed-ridden immobility for another two months. "Able to walk by the help of crutches," Solomon "hobbled down" to show an employee how to fix broken machinery of a saw-mill. But the unfortunate invalid "fell on the waterwheel, and bruised me most horribly. I was indeed helpless and in dreadful pain, confined month after month." Nor was this the end:

> I regained my strength so I could walk a little and ride side-ways. Soon after this I was wounded by a limb falling from a tree upon my head, which again nearly deprived me of life. I was carried in wholly unable to help myself.[37]

Solomon had one purpose in mentioning these catas-trophes, but they are reviewed now for another reason. After describing these three accidents, Solomon first refers to a possible convulsion: "I afterwards was taken with a fit." He obviously identified a cause and effect relationship between the brutal shocks to his system and nervous disorders that appeared "afterwards." Traveling alone in hill country when "the face of the land was covered with ice," Solomon "was senseless from one until five p.m." On regaining consciousness, "I had my axe still under my arm; I was all covered with blood and much cut and bruised." There were also "some fits" among his later disorders.[38] This much has supported an un-provable accusation against the disabled man. He was supposedly afflicted with hereditary epilepsy, which too neatly explains his grandson's visions as epileptic seizures, with flashing lights and lapses into unconsciousness.[39] But the case of neither grandfather nor grandson fits such speculation. Of Joseph Smith's significant visions, the majority involved others who viewed them simultaneously; nor did the Prophet generally experience loss of con-sciousness, and never injuries from a convulsion. More-over, each experience is recorded in detail as furnishing a coherent message, not a confused set of nervous impulses. As for Solomon Mack, any seizures appeared only after severe injuries and probably arose from neural damage. These facts do not support hereditary disorders. Diagnosis may be difficult enough with the living patient before the doctor. Both scientific and historical probabilities are violated by an arbitrary interpretation of Solomon Mack's physical symptoms and by bending the constitution of Joseph Smith to fit a theory.[40] This is a clever but inaccurate explanation of one who assumes that dreams and visions are automatic signs of abnormality.[41]

Injured or not, gritty Solomon refused to abandon an active life. At the close of the Revolution, he served on a privateer with two teenage sons, and the middle-aged man retained the cool courage of his youth. "We ship't aboard a privateer of 114 tons, commanded by Captain Havens," with a complement of about eighty men. Solomon tells of two engagements in the waters off Connecticut and Long Island. In the first, "five British privateers" drove his vessel "in upon Horseneck." There his crew mounted guns on shore, but their ship sustained heavy damage, its rigging cut away. After repairs they cast anchor offshore, and Solomon stood watch alone as others rested. "And very soon I espied two row-gallies, two sloops, two schooners; I rallied all hands on deck." With life again at stake, the American privateer made shore, and the crew barely had time to mount two guns on stern and two on a point of land. A furious cannonade began, followed by closer fighting. "One of the row-gallies went round the point of land to hem us in . . . but with our small arms we killed forty of the enemy." Such losses ended the attack: "they thought proper to leave us, pleased enough at the fight." Solomon remembered this combat "in the month of March," and on March 25, 1779, their exploits made news in the home port of New London:

A few days since, Capt. Havens, in the sloop Beaver, and Capt. Dennis, in a schooner, captured a schooner near Huntington, which they sent into Horseneck. The two privateers were soon after attacked by two row-gallies, who drove the Beaver on shore near Horseneck. But she was defended by her people till assisted by some Continental troops, who drove the gallies off. The Beaver had 3 or 4 of her people killed and several wounded.[42]

War hazards were followed by risks in seafaring. Solomon Mack had developed certain assets, for a letter came from Liverpool (a Nova Scotia port) "stating that a heavy debt that had been due me for a long time was collected and ready for me."[43] The father requested his oldest son to accompany him, which Jason did with extreme reluctance, for he was deeply in love and about to be married. The beginning of a touching tragedy, the journey of father and son was probably planned as a venture to invest in a ship and bring back trading profits to loved ones. But a rival suitor intercepted Jason's letters and after two years forged substitutes reporting Jason dead. His fiancée waited almost two years longer before unwittingly marrying the forger—only to collapse in frustration when her beloved shortly appeared. Jason went to sea again, to the sorrow of his parents. One can imagine the emotions of the wronged Macks—the mother who had so long believed the false notification, and the father who had urged his son to leave. Yet Solomon Mack writes of the event without a grudge, though aching in loneliness for news of his son:

But if this happens to meet the eye of the man who has brought this heavy affliction upon my boy and us his parents, I hope it may stimulate him to penitence and better deeds hereafter.[44]

The full story of four years at sea would have made a large book. Solomon began with fishing voyages off Nova Scotia, and his *Narrative* abbreviates "a terrible hurricane as ever I saw in my life"; masts were swept away, and all hands abandoned ship except "myself and my son."

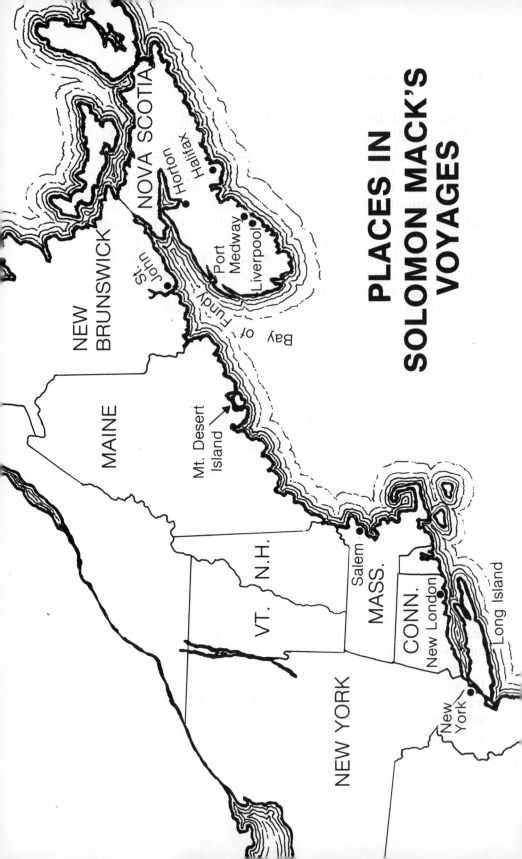

PLACES IN
SOLOMON MACK'S
VOYAGES

Solomon and Jason improvised rigging and worked the battered hull into port. After the owner repaired his schooner, Solomon bought it in a cash purchase. But the sea stalked his success. After escaping shipwreck by running before a December gale, he wintered at "Hawton" (evidently Horton, on the north coast of Nova Scotia), carrying passengers to Connecticut and returning "in the spring."[45] Next he "took in a freight of dry goods" at Halifax, bound westward around Nova Scotia for Horton: "On our passage we struck on a reef and employed other small vessels to take her loading and carry it to Liverpool harbor and secure it." A contemporary report of the Macks' grounded vessel appears in the diary of Simeon Perkins, prominent shipowner from Liverpool, who was temporarily in Halifax on business:

Wednesday, May 30th [1787]—Mr. Callahan, Spittenfield, and Dogget all arrive from Liverpool, and report that Jason Mack has stranded his vessel at Port Medway and lost a considerable quantity of goods, after they were saved out of the vessel. Mr. John Wm. Schwartz calls on me and desires me to take care of the goods, etc.[46]

The Macks floated their ship, but were "obliged to sell her to defray the expenses" of removing and securing the cargo. Not conceding defeat, Solomon labored until he "obtained the same vessel by honest industry." Master of a two-masted schooner of about forty tons capacity, he commanded a small crew and began "coasting," trading between ports in the Maritime Provinces and perhaps New England.[47] Determined not to return without profits, the seafarer stayed away until sickness drove him home empty-handed.

But the venturesome Solomon was richer in intangibles. If deprived of book learning, the Prophet's grandfather was no isolated farmer. He was already skilled in several vocations and well traveled for his time on land. In the years spanning the Revolution, he shipped into major ports from New York to Halifax. He now turned his back on the Atlantic with expanded horizons. The material world had been tested and found wanting. Solomon had toiled in youth and prime, only to have every surplus vanish, leaving no prospect of retirement: "but after all this earth, hard labor, and perplexity of mind, I had won nothing, and the best of my days were past." Such lessons were painful. "Late in the fall" Solomon put into Salem and lay sick for weeks; he "recovered and returned to my family after an absence of four years."[48]

Solomon rejoined his family in western Massachusetts. Early Revolutionary years had been spent in Gilsum, New Hampshire, where youngest child Lucy was born in 1775 and the mill accident probably took place in 1777. Next the Macks had moved some forty miles south to Montague, Massachusetts. Sons Jason and Stephen enlisted in that area in 1779, and daughter Lovisa married Joseph Tuttle there in 1780.[49] Reliable tradition from the Tuttles reveals some pride in their relationship to the Macks. Lovisa died without children, and Joseph remarried, passing on to his eldest son the following impressions:

> My father was twice married. His first wife was Lovice Mack, a daughter of old Capt. Mack, of Sunderland, Mass. Her father was an old sea captain and was well known in that vicinity.[50]

Solomon's four years at sea had been about 1784 to 1788.[51] He comments on the loss of "hundreds of dollars of my property" while away, and unjust creditors turned his family "out of doors" in his absence. Paul-like, Solomon Mack could be dejected and heroically persevere. He returned impoverished from the sea to an impoverished family; Solomon "now thought all was gone, and I did not care whether I lived or died." That was not wholly true, judged by the next thought: "but however, I went to work and shifted from plan to plan till at length I moved to Tunbridge in Vermont." A decade of labor is summarized in this sentence, and one "plan" was heavy construction. With access to Solomon's grandson, a competent local historian wrote:

Samuel Mack was a very ingenious mechanic, and with his brothers, Solomon and Elisha, was noted as a bridge and dam builder. He was the first man to build dams across the Connecticut River, and was employed by an English company to build one at Bellows Falls, where he was assisted by his brother Solomon, and *his* son Solomon, Jr.[52]

That location is doubtful, but immediate descendants evidently associated the Mack brothers on Connecticut River projects. The likely time would be the mutual years of Solomon and Elisha at Montague, Massachusetts, where both appear in the 1790 census. Elisha Mack's engineering exploits were legend in Montague and Greenfield, where he owned a sawmill. In 1792 the Massachusetts legislature authorized building and operating a toll bridge over the Connecticut River between Montague and Greenfield; Elisha Mack was one of the proprietors. The same session incorporated a group for developing locks and canals on the river, and Elisha had a leading role at Turners Falls:

The construction of the dam at Montague was first attempted some two miles below the falls, at Smead's Island, by Capt. Elisha Mack of Montague, who operated either as engineer for the corporation, or a contractor for its work. After a season of unsuccessful effort, the point was abandoned, chiefly on account of the depth of the water. In 1793, Capt. Mack succeeded in constructing a dam at Turners Falls. It stood one year on trial, as it was doubted whether it would be able to withstand the spring freshets, but it sustained the test.[53]

If Elisha and Solomon continued a working association that began with the grist and sawmill at Gilsum, New Hampshire, Solomon found returning there more congenial to his physical condition. From 1793 to 1797 Solomon Mack is found on the tax lists at Gilsum, where

THE CONNECTICUT RIVER AT SUNDERLAND, MASSACHUSETTS

he was probably farming, if not working again at the mills.[54] Daughter Lucy dated Solomon's return about 1792, and he traveled from there back to Massachusetts to see Lovisa in her dramatic last illness about 1794.[55] That was a year of personal tragedy, for he buried his two oldest daughters at Gilsum, though he could take comfort in the prosperous circumstances of his next daughter, Lydia, married in 1786 in that town to prominent Samuel Bill. Youngest daughter Lucy lived with her parents at Gilsum prior to her marriage in early 1796 and visited them there afterward.[56] About 1799 Solomon followed Lucy and his very successful son Stephen to Tunbridge, Vermont, where the father appears on the 1800 census. The story of this move is preserved in Solomon's recollection of "my passage" to Tunbridge. Too self-reliant for his safety, the spirited cripple insisted on driving cattle. Apparently on foot, he "fell and broke my wrist." If physical existence was painful, a lifetime of valor brought some security, for "by that time I had gained some property."[57] But more important to him was the spirituality of his ripe years, and he wrote to share this personal wealth.

While living in Vermont, Solomon Mack wrote his autobiography, with its motivation revealed in the subtitle: "An account of the many severe accidents he met with during a long series of years, together with the extraordinary manner in which he was converted to the Christian faith." Not aimlessly listing misfortunes, Solomon discerned that financial and physical setbacks had led him to higher things. In retrospect he saw himself as thoughtless of God, his protector in danger. Up to the reverses of middle-age, Solomon was unaware of his potential spirituality: "But strange to relate, and unaccountable as it may appear to a thinking mind, I never once thought on the God of my salvation or looked up to him for blessing or protection." Yet Solomon had been a highly moral man, strictly honest in his affairs and

generous to a fault with his means. Even in late Vermont
years, he paid "every farthing" when he "became bail
for a number of people."[58] But his futile quest for
material security had long forced him to question his
values. After seafaring years away from home, he resolved
to make amends: "I determined to follow phantoms no
longer, but devote the rest of my life to the service of
God and my family."[59] Only gradually, however, did
he understand:

> I had never read the Bible, nor had I any knowledge of it;
> could only recollect some taught parts such as I had heard and
> laid up for the purpose of ridiculing religious institutions and
> characters.[60]

Nevertheless Solomon Mack knew one of the great
invitations of the Lord: "Come unto me, all ye that labor
and are heavy laden, and I will give you rest."[61] Almost
eighty, Solomon lay confined with rheumatism for a
winter and reflected on his religious ignorance. Reference
to "so many warnings of my companion" indicates that
his wife had long sought to share what Solomon could
only find himself. In this winter of 1810-11 he "began to
search the Bible" and seriously question his wife, "my
only instructor." He tested the promise "ask, and it
shall be given you," and found his intense pain relieved
through prayer. More important, his dedicated search in
that winter brought peace of soul. There were some
manifestations—fully awake, he twice saw a light "as
bright as fire," and another time he heard a voice call
his name.[62] The great miracle, however, was the trans-
porting joy of his conversion:

> [E]verything appeared new and beautiful. Oh how I loved my
> neighbors. How I loved my enemies—I could pray for them.
> Everything appeared delightful. The love of Christ is beautiful.[63]

His profound joy is measured in the spontaneous
poetry that expressed faith and trust in the Savior. He

includes fourteen pages of his devotional hymns at the end of his pamphlet; if not displaying great literary ability, they burn with conviction. They express love of God, family, and fellowmen. The former sailor looks to his final harbor to "see my redeemer there"; the former soldier knows he is beyond the "warlike weapons" of evil. Immortality is a certainty, and his life a lesson:

> My friends, when you read this journal, remember your unfortunate friend Solomon Mack, who worried and toiled until an old age to try to lay up treasures in this world, but the Lord would not suffer me to have it. But now I trust I have treasures laid up that no man can take away—but by the goodness of God through the blood of a bleeding Savior.[64]

These words were written about 1811, and he had an active program for the closing nine years of life: "The remainder of my days, I mean to spend in my Father's service, though a poor cripple; cannot get on or off my horse without help."[65] All evidence from Solomon Mack's closing years shows that he carried out his intention to serve God full time after conversion. There were successful sons at Tunbridge, Vermont, but in 1804 he had moved from there, giving about $350 as payment on his 100-acre farm at Sharon, adjoining the town line of Royalton.[66] Soon this was rented to his son-in-law Joseph Smith, Sr., and was the Prophet's birthplace in 1805.[67] Before 1808 Joseph Smith's family had vacated this Sharon farm, and Solomon had moved back.[68] Not only did neighbors say so, but Solomon signed a deed on March 21, 1807, naming this land as "the farm that I now live on."[69] Solomon and wife were still living alone at Sharon when enumerated in the 1810 census.[70] In fact, on March 6, 1811, the town records there have this entry: "voted to exempt Mr. Solomon Mack from all taxes," probably because of the enervating sickness described by his *Narrative* as lasting until "the spring" of that year. By May 11, 1811, he was no longer bedridden— on that date Solomon Mack "of Sharon" sold his remaining interest in his farm for $500.[71]

This sale marked a new era in his life. Some proceeds must have defrayed the cost of printing his autobiography and testimony of conversion, published soon after he disposed of his land. This pamphlet was printed "at the expence of the author" at Windsor, some thirty-five miles away. Since it mentions riding his horse through neighboring towns, Solomon probably made the seventy-mile roundtrip to the printer on horseback, arranging for publication and later picking up the finished booklets. Memories of him persisted at Sharon and Royalton. A prominent neighbor was complimentary: "the elder Dewey often spoke of Solomon Mack, whom he knew, as being of a fine family."[72] One later ridiculed him as "an infirm man, who used to ride about the country on horseback, using . . . a 'side saddle.' "[73] Another could be more specific: "I well recollect Mr. Mack, . . . and his business on horseback was selling an autobiography of himself," a missionary activity judged by Solomon's convictions.[74]

About 1818 Solomon's wife died, perhaps precipitating a final move, for his concluding years were spent with his namesake-son, Solomon Mack, Jr.[75] So he finally returned to Gilsum, New Hampshire, where the 1819 assessor's list names no other taxable property but his horse.[76] But he is not listed in 1820, and his tombstone at Gilsum identifies that year as his last: "SOLOMON MACK, 1st. Died Aug. 23, 1820, AE. 84 ys."[77] His true age was nearly eighty-eight, but spirited Solomon had no concept of disability. He had written of his concern for the young:

> Parents, a little caution how to train up your children in the sight of the Lord. Never bid them to do anything that is out of their power, nor promise them only what you mean to fulfil. Set good examples in word, deed, and action.[78]

If the shadow of his youthful mistreatment falls over these words, his aged body housed a soul determined to give better than he received. That is the final mark of his long life:

> He . . . is remembered as riding about town on a side-saddle.
> . . . [H]e experienced a very remarkable religious conversion, and
> became very zealous, often visiting the schools and talking to the
> young on the subject of religion.[79]

Such religious conviction was inevitably shared with his
grandchildren. Especially intimate with his son-in-law
Joseph Smith, Sr., and daughter Lucy Mack Smith, Solomon Mack spent time with their children. Joseph Smith,
Jr., was an observant ten-year-old when his parents
moved to New York.[80]

History only incidentally records home life; yet there
are solid insights into the personalities of Joseph Smith's
grandmothers. They deserve final emphasis, since Joseph
Smith felt the impact of their immovable faith. One does
not read much of Lucy Mack Smith without sensing
the powerful relationship of the Prophet with his mother,
and no one influenced Lucy more than her own mother.
Lydia Gates was the oldest child of Daniel Gates
of East Haddam, Connecticut, the neighborhood of Solomon Mack's early Connecticut life. By tradition a tanner,
Daniel Gates is called "a man of wealth," and his estate
contained a substantial farm. His home provided a
Christian environment, for his children were baptized
shortly after birth, and Daniel is prominent in church
records as a deacon. His daughter Lydia completely accepted his religious convictions formalized in his will:

> I would . . . commit my soul into the hands of God, who gave
> it, hoping and believing that I shall obtain remission of all my sins
> through the alone merits of Jesus Christ, my only Savior, and that
> for his sake I shall be admitted into life eternal.[81]

Baptized as an infant, Lydia Gates made her own
profession of faith as an adult and was enrolled in the
Congregational Church.[82] Her religious life is vividly
portrayed in the writings of husband and daughter. Lucy
Mack Smith recalled a touching scene during her mother's
critical illness about 1784. Despairing of life, Lydia

gathered her family at her bedside to emphasize what she valued most. She encouraged her children "always to remember the instructions which she had given them— to fear God and walk uprightly before him." But she recovered to share three more decades of intimate companionship with Joseph Smith's mother. Lydia Gates Mack also deeply affected Solomon, who "had abused the Sabbath and had not taken warning from my wife."[83]

Before marriage Lydia Gates was "an amiable and accomplished young woman, a school teacher." Only afterward did Solomon appreciate the full influence of his wife. Not only did she exhibit "the polish of education, but she also possessed that inestimable jewel which in a wife and mother of a family is truly a pearl of great price, namely, a pious and devotional character."[84] Lydia's husband remembered vividly her moral leadership of the first decade of marriage, when the parents stood virtually alone against the wilderness at Marlow, New Hampshire. Lydia Mack endured inconvenience with "excellent disposition," but she also had ambition and capacity to educate her own:

> [A]s our children were deprived of schools, she assumed the charge of their education, and performed the duties of an instructress as none save a mother is capable of. Precepts accompanied with examples such as hers were calculated to make impressions on the minds of the young never to be forgotten.
>
> She, besides instructing them in the various branches of an ordinary education, was in the habit of calling them together both morning and evening and teaching them to pray, meanwhile urging upon them the necessity of love towards each other as well as devotional feelings towards him who made them. In this manner my first children became confirmed in habits of piety, gentleness, and reflection, which afforded great assistance in guiding those who came after them into the same happy channel.

Solomon perceived a significant fact about raising his family in the New Hampshire isolation of four families in forty miles. Since civilization's benefits were absent, so were its disadvantages. Home environment there had no rivals, so "their mother's precepts and example . . . had a more lasting influence upon their future character." With seasoned disdain of mere show, Solomon added that "all the flowery eloquence of the pulpit" could not have been as effective as his wife's influence, which included prayers that "came up daily before that all-seeing eye that rests upon all his works."[85]

Six children were trained by Lydia Mack in wilderness conditions at Marlow, New Hampshire; two more came after the Macks moved to nearby Gilsum. All eight are impressive evidence of the parents' leadership and example—youngest Lucy Mack Smith's opening chapters portray faith and generous concern as common traits of her brothers and sisters. Eldest Jason was a dynamic lay preacher who believed in miraculous healing, but also a practical leader of a successful cooperative settlement.[86] The eldest daughters possessed a sensitive devotion to each other and a faith that scorned death—chapter 4 reports their religious heroism under lengthy terminal sickness.[87] Remarkably like his father, Stephen Mack had spectacular farming and business success at Tunbridge, Vermont, and then became a major developer of early Detroit and Pontiac. At his death the *Detroit Gazette* emphasized his twenty-year Michigan residence; he was "distinguished from the mass of his fellow-citizens for his enterprise and the great utility of his views."[88] He was a pewholder in Tunbridge, Vermont, where his family generosity is measured by the $1,000 wedding gift to Lucy Smith from him and his business partner. Another venturesome temperament was Daniel, and glimpses of his life remain—Lucy Mack Smith relates his rescue of three men from drowning in explaining his "very daring and philanthropic spirit." The same phrase describes Lucy herself, who fervently sought God and stood courageously by her convictions before and after accepting the revelations of her son Joseph Smith, Jr. The remaining two Mack children settled in Gilsum, New

Hampshire. They were affluent in this community, but they remembered God and fellowmen. Solomon Mack, Jr., was a successful farmer and community leader, holding positions in town government and militia. When he was seventy, Hyrum Smith visited him and reported: "Uncle Solomon seemed to be lively and cheerful, and quite thoughtful about his future state."[89] Lydia Mack's marriage to prosperous Samuel Bill has been noted; Lucy Smith insists that "she dealt out her substance to the needy with a liberal hand to the end of her days." Lydia Mack Bill's gravestone symbolizes the Christian commitment that her mother Lydia effectively bequeathed:

> Now she's gone to realms above,
>   Where saints and angels meet;
> To realize her Savior's love
>   And worship at his feet.[90]

The Mack sons and daughters are realities reflecting the intense conviction of Lydia Gates Mack. Joseph Smith, Jr., also came under his grandmother's influence, for he remembered her presence as the Smiths began their journey to New York.[91] The Prophet's mother also mentions that "my aged mother . . . had lived with us some time."[92] But accompanying the emigrants a short distance, Lydia Gates Mack was injured by an overturning wagon.[93] She accurately sensed that she would not live much longer and wept at parting. Her daughter's thoughts at that moment epitomize a heritage: "I was here to take leave of that pious and affectionate parent to whom I was indebted for all the religious instructions as well as most of the educational privileges which I had ever received." In turn, the aged mother's first concern was reiterating her faith, so resolutely preserved for further generations:

I must soon exchange the things of earth for another state of existence, where I hope to enjoy the society of the blessed. And now, as my last admonition, I beseech you to continue faithful in the exercise of every religious duty to the end of your days, that I may have the pleasure of embracing you in another fairer world above.[94]

CHAPTER 3

Writings of Solomon Mack

Solomon Mack's known writings come from his auto-biography, written late, probably the spring of 1811 (see n. 3). Lucy Smith appears to use a fuller manuscript of her father, since she quotes unpublished episodes from her father in the first person (see n. 29 and n. 44). One suspects that Solomon kept a rather extensive journal, from which his *Narrative* was extracted, but it is the autobiography proper that is fully reprinted here. This includes some two dozen pages of the original edition plus two pages of "errata" appended by the author. Paging of the original is preserved, indicated in brackets at the top of each page of the *Narrative*. Solomon Mack added nineteen pages of verse to his autobiography, de-votional poetry expressing faith and gratitude for his conversion, and selections from this material follow his life story.

The remaining small portion of Solomon's pamphlet is reserved for reprinting in the following chapter. This is his two-page narrative of daughter Lovisa's sickness and death, and it is separately printed for comparison with Lucy Mack Smith's similar account. Thus all of Solomon Mack's printed prose appears here. The close of the addition on Lovisa restates the conclusion of the autobiography proper, and was intended as the final in-junction of the pamphlet:

My friends, when you read this journal, remember your un-fortunate friend Solomon Mack, who worried and toiled until an old age to try to lay up treasures in this world, but the Lord would not suffer me to have it. But now I trust I have treasures laid up that no man can take away—but by the goodness of God through the blood of a bleeding Savior.

Although I am a poor cripple, unable to walk much or even to mount or dismount my horse, I hope to serve my God, by his assistance to divine acceptance, that I may at last leap for joy to see his face and hold him fast in my embrace.

Reprinting a work published over 150 years ago makes rivals of accuracy and readability. Because early type faces can be confusing, photographic reproduction is impractical. Spelling errors are corrected, but forms correct in Solomon's day are largely untouched—yet certain patterns have been regularized where the first printing was not wholly consistent with itself. Abbreviations have generally been written out, and geographical names spelled according to accepted usage. There is no question of ambiguity, except where "St. John's" has been changed to "St. John," the latter New Brunswick location more in accord with Solomon's narrative than the Newfoundland city. "Hawton" is changed to "Horton" with little possibility of error (n. 45). Personal names have occasionally been regularized, but one suspects that the typesetter did not always read Mack's manuscript correctly. Fellow-soldier "Bowley" (p. [8]) is actually Rowley (n. 23); the Mohawk chief Hendrick appears as "Kenrick" (p. [47]); and the census records of Surry, New Hampshire, show that Samuel McCordy lived there instead of the "Samuel M. Cordy" of the pamphlet (p. [17]), corresponding with John McCurdy, the brother and estate administrator also mentioned (pp. [16-17] and n. 51). This notation is made for these men, however, instead of the rather clumsy repeated bracketing of the names. Little has been modified in editing by the rules just mentioned, and anything added is indicated in brackets, the standard sign for editorial modification. The only extensive changes are in capitalization and punctuation, where editorial duty dictates readable copy. Original punctuation and capitalization have been changed cautiously, seeking clarity by breaking down sentences into more readable units.

A

NARRAITVE

OF THE LIFE OF

SOLOMON MACK,

CONTAINING·

AN ACCOUNT

OF THE MANY SEVERE ACCIDENTS HE MET
WITH DURING A LONG SERIES OF YEARS,

TOGETHER WITH

THE EXTRAORDINARY MANNER IN
WHICH HE WAS CONVERTED TO THE

CHRISTIAN FAITH.

—◦—

TO WHICH IS ADDED,
A NUMBER HYMNS COMPOSED ON THE
DEATH OF SEVERAL OF HIS
RELATIONS.

WINDSOR.
PRINTED AT THE EXPENCE OF THE
AUTHOR.

[3]

I, SOLOMON MACK, was born in Connecticut, in the town of Lyme near the mouth
of Connecticut River, September 26, 1735,
my parents, Ebenezer and Hannah Mack.
Ebenezer Mack departed this life in 1777.
He went to the door to fetch in a back-log
and returned after a fore-stick and instantly
dropped down dead on the floor. You may see by
this our lives are dependent on a supreme and
independent God. Hannah Mack departed this
life in 1796 with a long fit of sickness;
she experienced the power of God from an early
age, with all the good morals of life, and
instructing the youth for about thirty years.
She died rejoicing and wishing her last moments
to come. Rejoicing she went home to meet her
Father in the realms of eternal bliss.
    My parents had a large property and lived
in good style. From various misfortunes, and
the more complicated evils attendant on the
depravity of the sons of men, my parents became poor. And when I was four years old the
family, then consisting of five children, were
obliged to disperse and throw themselves upon
the mercy of an unfeeling and evil world.
I was bound out to a farmer in the neighborhood. As is too commonly the case, I was
rather considered as a slave than a member of
the family. And instead of allowing me the privilege of common hospitality and a claim to

[4]

that kind protection due to the helpless and in-
digent children, I was treated by my master as
his property and not as his fellow mortal. He
taught me to work and was very careful that
I should have little or no rest. From labor
he never taught me to read or spoke to me at
all on the subject of religion. His whole attention was taken up on the pursuits of the
good things of this world; wealth was his supreme object. I am afraid gold was his God,
or rather he never conversed on any other subject. And I must say he lived without God in
the world, and to all appearance God was not
in his thoughts.

I lived with this man (whose name, for
many reasons, I did not think proper to mention)
until I was 21 years of age lacking 2 months,
when a difficulty took place between me and
my master, which terminated in our separation
at that time. I, however, at his request returned and fulfilled the indenture; which in consequence of being frequently abused, I had
found my indentures in my master's custody,
and I burnt them. My mistress was afraid of
my commencing a suit against them, she took
me aside and told me I was such a fool we could
not learn you. I was totally ignorant of divine revelation or anything appertaining to
the Christian religion. I was never taught even
the principles of common morality and felt no
obligation with regard to society and was born

[5]

as others, like the wild ass's colt. I met with
many sore accidents during the years of my min-
ority.

I had a terrible fever sore on my leg which
had well nigh proved fatal to my life, which it
seems was occasioned by a scald that terminated
in a severe fit of sickness. In these trials my
master was very kind to me. He procured the
best physicians and surgeons and provided everything necessary for my comfort, all which as
I suppose that he might again reap the benefit
of my labor. For although it was thought for
a time that I could not live, yet my master never spoke to me of death, judgment or eternity; nor did he ever to my recollection discover
that he himself had any idea that he was made
to die, or that he had here no continuing city,
or ever thought of seeking one to come.

Soon after I left my master, I enlisted in the
service of my country under the command of
Captain Henry and was annexed to a regiment
commanded by Colonel Whiting. I marched from
Connecticut to Fort Edward; there was a severe
battle fought at the Halfway Brook in the
year 1755.

I had been out a long scout, and I caught a
bad cold and was taken sick and remained so
all the rest of the winter. And in the spring,
1756, I was carried to Albany in a wagon,
where I saw five men hung at one time. I remained sick the biggest part of the summer. I went

[Compare this page with final ERRATA.]

[6]

to Lyme and purchased a farm. In the year
1757 I mustered two teams in the King's service for one season. I then went to Stillwater
with the general's baggage. One morning I
went out to yoke up as usual and found there
was three of my oxen missing; the officer was
so angry that he drew his sword to run me
through but immediately exclaimed, get thee
out three of any you can find, which I accordingly did. Then I went on with the baggage and arrived at Fort Edward; then I returned back after my oxen. When I got about
halfway I espied at about thirty rods distance,
four Indians coming out of the woods with
their tomahawks, scalping-knives and guns.
I was alone, but about twenty rods behind me
there was a man by the name of Webster. I
saw no other way to save myself only to deceive
them by stratagem. I exclaimed like this:
*Rush on! Rush on! Brave boys, we'll have the
devils! We'll have the devils!* I had no other
weapon only a staff. But I ran towards them,
and the other man appearing in sight, gave
them a terrible fright, and I saw them no more.
But I am bound to say the grass did not grow
under my feet.

I hastened to Stillwater and found my oxen;
the same night I returned back through the
woods alone, which was about seven miles.
The next morning I was ready to go on my
journey again. From thence I went to Lake

[7]

George. I followed teaming the remainder of
the season, but by accident I was taken with the
smallpox at Albany. I entrusted a man to
convey my teams to Litchfield and gave him
15 dollars for his services. But instead of
doing as he agreed, he went twenty miles and
sold one team, then went a short distance and
left the other. But after I regained my health
I went and bought them again and returned to
Lyme.

Soon after I enlisted under Major Spencer
in 1758, and went over the lakes. There was
a severe battle fought; Lord Howe was killed.
His bowels were taken out and were buried; his
body was embalmed and carried to England.

The next day we marched to the breastworks
and were obliged to retreat with the loss of
five hundred killed and as many more wounded.
But I escaped very narrowly by a musket ball
passing under my chin, perhaps within half
an inch of my neck. In this rencontre I had
no reflection, only that I thought I had by my
good luck escaped a narrow shot. The army
returned back to Lake George. A large scouting party of the enemy came round by Skenesborough, at the Halfway Brook, and cut off
a large number of our men and teams. One
thousand of our men set out to go to Skenesborough after the enemy; five hundred of
them were sent back. And just as we got to
South Bay the enemy got out of our reach.

[8]

The enemy went to Ticonderoga and got recruited; they then came after us. We scouted by
Wood Creek. On the 13th day we got to Fort
Ann. The sentry came and told me that the
enemy was all around us. Major Putnam led
out the party. Major Rogers bro't up the rear,
marched in an Indian path three-quarters of a
mile. The Indians lay in a half-moon. Major
Putnam went through their ranks; they fired
upon us. Major Putnam was taken and tied
to a tree, and an Indian would have killed him
had it not been for a French lieutenant who
rescued his life. The enemy rose like a cloud
and fired a volley upon us, and my being in the
front brought me into the rear. I turned little
to the right, the tomahawks and bullets flying
around my ears like hailstones. And as I was
running, I saw a great windfall little forward
which seemed impossible for me or any other
man to mount, but over I went. And as I ran I
looked little one side, where I saw a man wounded (the Indians close to him), who immediately
with my help got into the circle. Gershom
[R]owley had nine bullets shot thro' his clothes
and remained unhurt. Ensign Worcester had
nine wounds, scalped and tomahawked, who lived
and got well.

The battle commenced in the morning and
continued until three o'clock, when they left
us. We gathered our dead and wounded up in
a ring; there was half of our men killed and

[9]

wounded and taken. We sent to Fort Edward
for relief to help carry our wounded, it being
80 in number; we made biers to carry them,
many of whom died on the passage, the distance
being 14 miles.

I was almost beat out, but I went to Albany
after stores and returned to the army. From
thence I went home, it being in the fall, and
tarried through the winter.

In the spring, 1754, I set out on another
campaign. I went to Crown Point, and there
I set up a sutler's shop, which I kept two years
by means of a clerk I employed for that purpose,
not knowing myself how to write or read to
any amount what others had written or printed.
I lost my clerk, and not being able properly
to adjust accounts, lost what I had accumulated
by hard industry for several years, all for
the want of youthful education.

After leaving the army I accumulated by
industry a handsome sum of silver and gold.
With it I purchased in the town of Granville
sixteen hundred acres of land and paid for it
on delivery of the deed—but besides I was to
clear a small piece of land on each right and
build a log house. But previous to this I married in the year 1761.

I then proceeded into the back country to
clear me a farm. Soon after I began to work in
the woods, but unfortunately cut my leg and
lay under the doctor's care the whole season,

[Compare this page with final ERRATA.]

[10]

which cost me a large sum and well nigh took
my life. I underwent everything but death,
but thought nothing of the hand that inflicted
the chastisement. My family arrived, and we
were in the wilderness and could do no business. Previous to this, however, I freighted a
vessel and went to New York, where I sold my
cargo extremely high, and returning was overtaken by a gale of wind. My vessel was much
damaged, but we made shift and got to Long
Island, and there we left the vessel.

I arrived at home sometime in the winter,
poor enough; the vessel did not arrive till the
next spring. Afterwards I broke my wrist,
with which I had a great deal of pain and expense. For a long time I was unable to do any
labor. Though I still sought to make myself
great and happy in the way I was educated,
the Lord would not suffer me to prosper. I
was not yet discouraged. Soon after I went
to Moodus and learnt of my brother-in-law
how to make saltpeter. Though being a cripple, I went to Old Springfield and Longmeadow
to show them the art of making saltpeter.
I was sent for from town to town; my wages
was one dollar per day. This was in our
Revolutionary War. I then enlisted into the
American army. I soon mustered two teams
and carried baggage to Skenesborough. I
afterwards enlisted into a company of artillery
for a short campaign, but on my return home

[11]

I was taken sick. As soon as I recovered I went
to see my son. He was cutting trees, when unfortunately a tree fell on me and crushed me
almost all to pieces—beat the breath out of my
body. My son took me up for dead. I, however,
soon recovered, but have not to this day recovered the use of my limbs, which was 34 years
ago. I lay sixty days on my back and never
moved or turned to one side or the other.
The skin was worn off my back from one end
to the other. I was then taken by six men in
a sheet and moved from time to time for sixty
or seventy days more, when I was able to walk
by the help of crutches. I had a man to work
in a saw-mill; it got out of order. I hobbled
down to show him how to mend it, and by accident I fell on the waterwheel and bruised
me most horribly. I was indeed helpless and
in dreadful pain, confined month after month,
unable to help myself. But at last I was restored
to health, but being destitute of property and
without my natural strength to get my bread,
with a young and dependent family whose
daily wants were increasing and none to administer relief. But strange to relate and unaccountable as it may appear to a thinking
mind, I never once thought on the God of my
salvation or looked up to him for blessing or
protection; I was stupid and thoughtless.
   Owing to my misfortune I could not attend to my contract at Granville, so I lost all

[12]

my land; however, I regained my strength so
I could walk a little and ride sideways. Soon
after this I was wounded by a limb falling from
a tree upon my head, which again nearly deprived
me of life. I was carried in wholly unable to
help myself. I, however, recovered again; I
can say like this: the time of my departure
was not yet come, and there was yet more
trouble for me to pass through.

I afterwards was taken with a fit, when
traveling with an axe under my arm on Winchester hills; the face of the land was covered with ice. I was senseless from one until
five p.m. When I came to myself I had my
axe still under my arm; I was all covered
with blood and much cut and bruised. When
I came to my senses I could not tell where
I had been nor where I was going. But by good
luck I went right and arrived at the first
house—was under the doctor's care all the winter.
In the next place I fell[ed] seven large
trees against another, and very imprudently
went to cut away the prop—when suddenly the
whole fell together, and I in the midst of
them. This time I remained unhurt but thought
nothing of the power that protected me, blind
as ever.

Soon after I and my two sons went out
a-privateering. We ship't aboard a privateer
of 114 tons, commanded by Captain Havens;
there was about eighty men on board. We

[13]

were chased by five British privateers; they
drove us in upon Horseneck, where we got
some of our guns on shore; we brought them
to bear upon the enemy. We exchanged a great
many shots; they shattered our vessel and
cut away our rigging. The next day our officers went up into town, and five repaired our
vessel; then hauled off from the wharf; then
cast anchor. Every man on board went to their
rest except myself, in the month of March. And
very soon I espied two row-gallies, two sloops,
two schooners; I rallied all hands on deck.
They quick obeyed, and we weighed anchor—
then hauled by the side of the wharf but had
only time to get two cannon out on the point
of land and two on the stern of the vessel.
This engagement began in the morning. The enemy
gave us a broadside, and where the bullets
struck, it had the appearance of a furrow made
by a plough. Staddles in gun shot was all cut
asunder. One of the row-gallies went round
the point of land to hem us in, and they had
near ran aground, but with our small arms we
killed forty of the enemy. We sent our cabin
boys up to a house near the shore with a wounded man. Just as the boys entered the door there
came an eighteen pounder into the house, and the
woman was frying cakes over the fire. Says
the woman to the boys, take the cakes, and
I will go down cellar. By our killing
so many of the enemy they thought proper to

[14]

leave us, pleased enough at the fight. For if
we had been taken, what would our punishment have
been. But I thought nothing of futurity, which
if I had considered a moment and viewed a
watery grave already made, it appears as if
I must have shuddered at the thought. My God
must have given me some warnings of my danger,
but if he did, his calls I would not hearken
to. The devil had great hold on me, and I
served him well. But the Lord was with me—
yes, he has supported me to this day through
trials and fatigues. But now I feel to sing
praises with the celestial bands above.
How thankful, my friends, I am to join with
Christian friends now in my old age, but I
must leave this subject.
    Next we hoisted sail and made for New
London. After the war we freighted a vessel
and went to Liverpool and sold our loading and
ship't aboard Captain Foster's and went [on] a
fishing voyage. And so I went two voyage[s],
and the third voyage I was in the cabin when I
heard a rout on deck. I sprang up as quick as
possible, and there being a terrible hurricane
as ever I saw in my life. Both masts was carried
overboard, and if they had not we must all have found
watery graves—we ought to have been thankful and
bless the Lord for it. Our captain and all
hands appeared to be greatly surprised, but
we was all spared through the tempest. We
ought to be thankful to our God for a few moments

A SCHOONER IN STORMY SEAS, BY WINSLOW HOMER

[15]

for repentance, but we thought nothing of
these things.

The hands all left her but myself and my
son. We stuck fast by the hull, and that night
we caught 25 large fish; but by jury masts we
worked her into Liverpool. We went on board
another vessel and sailed for Halifax. Mean-
while Captain Foster repaired his schooner and
proceeded to Halifax, and there he found me.
I bought his vessel, and by good fortune I was
able to pay the whole purchase except eight
pounds. I then took a freight and went to St.
[John], and on our return to Halifax we were
overtaken by a gale of wind and well nigh lost
all hands, vessel and cargo. We, however, made for
Mount Desert and obtained it. I was very uneasy
about my property but thought of nothing else.
We repaired our vessel and returned to Halifax;
this was the first of January. Such a day I
never saw before nor since—nothing but confusion.
Almost every sailor was intoxicated, myself
amongst the rest. After I came to myself I reflected a little on such conduct, resolving to
amend from such practices. But soon I forgot
amidst the bustle of the world.

The next day I sailed up the bay of Fundy
and wintered at [Horton]. There I made an agreement to take thirty passengers on board (at
eight dollars per head) and carried them to
New London and brought them back again in

[16]

the spring. So I returned to Halifax and took
in a freight of dry goods, and again sailed for
[Horton]. On our passage we struck on a reef
and employed other small vessels to take her
loading and carry it to Liverpool harbor and
secure it; and then I informed the sundry
owners of the circumstance. But I soon got my
vessel off again, but it cost me one dollar an
hour for each man. The cost being so much, I
was obliged to sell her to defray the expenses.
Again I was left destitute of property.

I had by this time recovered my health, and
was not willing to return empty. I immediately
went to work and again obtained the same vessel
by honest industry. My next business was to
follow coasting, but late in the fall I landed
at Salem and was taken very sick. I lay there
some weeks, when I recovered and returned to
my family after an absence of four years, in
which time I had not heard from them. I had
very little property, and my family had been
turned out of doors on account of placing confidence in those that I took to be my friends.
But by unjust dealing they took hundreds of
dollars of my property. When I went from home
I owed John Cordy at Lyme one hundred dollars; Nathaniel Peck of Lyme owed me one hundred dollars. He gave me a note; I gave that
note to John Cordy to pay that debt. Nathaniel Peck went to sea and died. John Cordy
administer[ed] upon Nathaniel Peck's estate.

[17]

Mr. Cordy got just d.26,66 of his debt. Mr.
Cordy came up here and asked me if I would let
his brother Samuel take the note; I gave him
leave. I then drove two yoke of oxen to Samuel
M. Cordy, Surry. Those oxen with the d.26,66
paid the debt. John Cordy at Lyme did not know
it, and on his deathbed he willed me half of
the said debt (his widow and son signed the
will). Likewise, when I was at sea Samuel M.
Cordy got all the writings and turned my family
out of doors.

    This I can prove by Abisha Tubbs, Esq.
Kind reader, look at the nature of mankind,
what they will do for silver and gold. But
after all this earth, hard labor and perplexity
of mind, I had won nothing—and the best of my
days were past and gone and had to begin entirely
anew. I now thought all was gone, and I
did not care whether I lived or died. But
however, I went to work and shifted from plan
to plan till at length I moved to Tunbridge, in
Vermont. On my passage I undertook driving
cattle, but by accident I fell and broke my
wrist. I walked eight miles before I could
get it set. By that time I had gained some
property, altho I was all this time a cripple
and afflicted with broken bones and sore sicknesses
and some fits. To add to all the rest, I became
bail for a number of people, and all that I was
bondman for, and took all I had. I had to pay

[18]

every farthing, and it reduced me to poverty
again, in advanced age without the means of
hiring or anyone to relieve our wants. Who
is able or willing to bear our burden?
　　A few particulars which were forgotten.
As I was passing through Woodstock, a number
of troopers rode by in haste, struck my side, my
horse run, and I immediately fell backwards and
almost was killed; and I did not recover for a
number of months. At another time I fell and
broke my shoulder. At another time at [Hor-
ton], I was riding in the road; a boy in making his obeisance, started my horse, and I fell
to the ground and was much bruised. At another
time at Royalton my horse fell, and through
the mercy of God my life was spared and not
much hurt. At another time I fell in a fit
at Tunbridge, and was supported for the
benefit of my soul and others. In the fall of
the year 1810, in the 76th year of my age, I
was taken with the rheumatism, and confined me
all winter in the most extreme pain for most
of the time. I under affliction and dispensation
of providence, at length began to consider my
ways and found myself destitute of knowledge
to extol me to enquire. I thought on the best
that is recorded in the 11th chapter of Matthew, and 28th to the 30th verses came to my
mind. I asked my wife whether those words
were in the Bible or not. She told me they were.
That gave me a shock, and very uneasy I was, not

[19]

knowing where they were. I began to search
the Bible. But often before this I had trials,
but I would not hearken. I had practically said
unto God, depart from me—I desire not the knowledge of thy ways. I had all my days set at
naught his councils and words. I often slighted
till an advanced age, but now I experienced personal deliverance. Yet I had all these number of
years been totally blind to the things that
belonged to my peace. I had fears and put up
prayers before God in this situation. I had
incurred (as I thought) the denunciation: I
will pour out my fury upon the heathen and upon
the families that call not on my name.
   My mind was imagining, but agitated I
imagined many things. It seemed to me that I
saw a bright light in a dark night when contemplating on my bed, which I could not account for—but I thought I heard a voice
calling to me again. I thought I saw another
light of the same kind, all which I considered
as ominous of my own dissolution. I was in
distress, that sleep departed from my eyes;
and I literally watered my pillow with tears,
that I prayed eagerly that God would have
mercy on me, that he would relieve me and
open the eyes of my understanding and enable
me to call on him as I ought. It brought passages of scripture to my mind, those particular.
Christ's lamentations over Jerusalem struck me
very forcibly to think that often the Lord had

[20]

called, and I was stubborn and would not; therefore
I [was] left desolate. The whole force of the scripture seemed to be out against me as far as I could
learn. My wife was my only instructor. I had
never read the Bible, nor had I any knowledge
of it; could only recollect some taught parts
such as I had heard and laid up for the purpose
of ridiculing religious institutions and characters. I, however, had my intention. I believe
these things have turned to my advantage, but I
hope and trust I found mercy. I do believe that
God did appear for me and took me out of the
horrible pit and mirey clay, and set my feet on
the rock of Christ Jesus. Blessed be the name
of Jehovah, that I have reason to hope that I
have found him of whom the prophets did write,
and that he has told me all things that ever I
did, has enabled me to cast my burthen on the
Lord and to believe that he will sustain me,
to whom be glory for ever and ever.

A few words upon the universal principle—
I have experienced it through the early part of
my life, but I say it was like building on sand.
A certain learned man built seven years upon
it, but upon his death bed he damned the principle and made this reply, "I shall be damned
to all eternity for this principle." He went
out of the world smiting his fists almost in
despair, and I having no learning, thinking of him

[21]

who made me believe it would deceive me. I
have tried and reached much after property
and several times obtained it, but by misfortunes time after time I lost it. I at length
got wholly discouraged of trying to lay up on
earth, where moth and rust doth corrupt, and
thieves break through and steal, which put me
to thinking something of death and eternity
till I thought myself almost a Christian and
was so religious that I once went to talk with
a sick man on his death bed. But if the Lord
had taken me away with such false hopes, I
should have been miserable to all eternity.
This is Universalists that I am speaking of.
This will not answer, deceived man and woman.
Last fall I was again almost a Christian, but
I found it would not answer to depend on such
foundation. Those verses still run in my mind,
Matthew, the 11th chapter and 28th, 29th verses:
Come unto me all ye that labor and are heavy
laden, and I will give you rest. Take my yoke
upon you, and learn of me, for I am meek and
lowly in heart, and ye shall find rest unto
your souls. For my yoke is easy, and my burthen
is light.

I was so stupid that I did not know whether
these words were in the Bible or not; I asked
my wife, and she told me they were and where
they were. I then discovered how ignorant and
stupid I had been even to a great age. And I saw
what offers of mercy I had, but I slighted

[22]

them. It brought to my mind Christ's sayings
in St. Matthew, 23d chapter and 37th verse:
O Jerusalem, thou that killest the prophets and
stonest them that are sent unto thee; how often
would I have gathered thy children together
even as the hen gathereth her chickens under
her wings, and ye would not. Reader, you
may think I was in great distress. I could not
sleep and took to reading. I was distressed
to think how I had abused the Sabbath and had
not taken warning from my wife. About mid-
night I saw a light about a foot from my face
as bright as fire; the doors were all shut and
no one stirring in the house. I thought by this
that I had but a few moments to live, and oh
what distress I was in. I prayed that the Lord
would have mercy on my soul and deliver me from
this horrible pit of sin. I thought myself that
I had been such a vile wretch that the Lord
would not have mercy on me, and I thought as I
had slighted so many warnings from my companion and so abused the Sabbath; but I perceived my body and soul was in danger; oh
reader, you may think I was in distress.
　Another night soon after, I saw another light
as bright as the first, at a small distance from
my face, and I thought I had but a few moments
to live. And not sleeping nights and reading, all day I was in misery; well you may
think I was in distress, soul and body. At another time in the dead of the night I was called

[23]

by my Christian name; I arise up to answer to
my name. The doors all being shut and the
house still, I thought the Lord called, and I had
but a moment to live. Oh what a vile wretch
I had been. I prayed to the Lord to have
mercy on my soul. I called upon the Lord
the greatest part of the winter, and towards
spring it was reviving and light shined into
my soul. I have often thought that the lights
which I saw were to show me what a situation
I was in. I had slighted his calls and invitations
and warnings from my companion, and what a
sandy foundation I was on. The calls, I believe,
were for me to return to the Lord, who would
have mercy on me.

All the winter I was laid up with the rheumatism, so that my wife was obliged to help
me to bed and up again, but in the spring the
Lord appeared to be with me. But for my own
satisfaction, I thought like this, as I was sitting one evening by the fire. I prayed to the
Lord, if he was with me, that I might know it by
this token—that my pains might all be eased for
that night. And blessed be the Lord, I was entirely free from pain that night. And I rejoiced
in the God of my salvation—and found Christ's
promises verified that what things soever ye
ask in prayer, believing, ye shall receive—and
found that Christ would fulfil all his promises,
and not one jot or tittle would fail. And the
Lord so shined light into my soul that every-

[24]

thing appeared new and beautiful. Oh how
I loved my neighbors. How I loved my enemies—
I could pray for them. Everything appeared
delightful. The love of Christ is beautiful.
There is more satisfaction to be taken in the
enjoyment of Christ one day, than in half a
century serving our master, the devil. You
that have children under your care that have no
parents, when you put anything upon them
to do, consider them as your own, that when
death overtakes you, you need not fear their
apparitions appearing in your sight for
tyranny and misusage of the fatherless and
motherless. Time will come when we shall
all be called for, sooner or later, when money
cannot buy our breath one moment. Parents,
a little caution how to train up your children
in the sight of the Lord. Never bid them to
do anything that is out of their power, nor
promise them only what you mean to fulfil.
Set good examples in word, deed, and action.
We aged parents have a Father to go to and
to guide us if we will but obey and hearken to
his calls. How often we hear, but do not
obey him. But why? Because we will say there
is time enough yet, and I have something more
to attend to of my worldly business. But how
am I bringing up my children, in the fear of
the Lord? I answer no, but in all manner of
evils, Sabbath breaking, lying, swearing, etc.,
giving them no counsels from the command of

[25]

our God. Bless the rising generation with his
outpouring from corner to corner. I invite
you to hearken to the calls that often presses
into your minds, and put it not away for another
day. I give you a weak advice; I am almost
brought to the ground with sore accidents, and
greatly advanced in years. I always lived in
sin, an enemy to God till in my seventy-sixth
year. Then I began to hearken to these calls—
made alive through the blessedness of Christ—
reconciled to God. Oh my friends, what views
I had—the love I had to God and my fellow
mortals, I cannot express.

The remainder of my days, I mean to spend
in my Father's service, though a poor cripple;
cannot get on or off my horse without help. I
have a love to all: rich and poor, kings and
nobles, black and white. Come all to Jesus,
my friends, come to Jesus, and he will in no
wise cast you off. Oh, come, come; how sweet
is the love to Jesus—how beautiful is the
love of God. This invitation is from my heart
to hear of your repenting and turning to my
God. Take no pattern from me, for I would
not hearken till I arrived to advanced age—
swared from time to time; now I have a love for
your souls. Now listen to me, though like a
child, but shun that path that I used to walk
in—this is the prayer of SOLOMON MACK.

[47, 48]

ERRATA

In the year 1755, I enlisted under Captain
Harris and went to Fort Edward. There was a
large army come from South Bay (now called
Skenesborough) upon a scouting party of our
men at Halfway Brook. There was a scouting
party of the enemy attacked our men, and [Hen-
drick's] horse was shot under him, and he was
killed. When they heard the guns, General Lyman
and Colonel Johnson had not a log put up. The
enemy fought seven miles and killed them all
the way. When they got there the breast work
was finished. This battle lasted all day; many
were killed on both sides. The remainder of
the enemy went back to Halfway Brook (being
seven miles) and refreshed themselves upon
their spoil. Then a party of New Hampshire
troops come upon them and killed a great number
of them. I was married in the year 1759, instead of
21—same page, instead of 1754, 1759. Then I
went to Crown Point and kept a sutler's shop
27 years. In the year 1757 a large army came
from Quebec and took Fort William Henry. The
French guarded the prisoners fourteen miles.
The blood-thirsty Indians kept breaking in upon
the guard and killing them all the way.

[The printed numbers "[17]21" and "27"
are obvious errors.]

SOLOMON MACK'S VERSE

Solomon Mack did not claim to write poetry, but did
express his love for God in what he titles "hymns, composed and selected on different occasions." Presumably
those "selected" are the two long expressions of faith of
his sisters, and the remaining ones are his own composition. The first two and last two are printed here, all but
the second untitled. The seven compositions not reproduced tend to restate the themes of these four, chosen
partly for brevity and partly for biographical interest.

> My friends, I am on the ocean,
>   So sweetly do I sail.
> Jesus he is my portion;
>   He's given me a pleasant gale.
>
> The bruises sore;
>   In harbour soon I'll be,
> And see my redeemer there
>   That died for you and me.

Psalm for Deliverance from Great Distress

> I waited patient on the Lord;   *very similar*
>   He bowed to hear my cry.   *to psalm*
> He saw me resting on his word
>   And brought salvation nigh.
>
> He rais'd me from a horrid pit
>   Where mourning long I lay,
> And from my bonds releas'd my feet,
>   Deep bonds of mirey clay.
>
> Firm on a rock he made me stand,
>   And taught my cheerful tongue
> To praise the wonders of his hand,
>   In a new thankful song.
>
> I'll spread his works of grace abroad;
>   The saints with joy shall hear,
> And sinners learn to make my God
>   Their only hope and fear.

How many are thy thoughts of love!
    Thy mercies, Lord, how great!
We have not words nor hours enough
    Their numbers to repeat.

When I'm afflicted, poor and low,
    And light and peace depart;
My God beholds my heavy woe,
    And bears me on his heart.

Jesus is mine, and I am his;
    In union we are joined.
Oh how sweet to me it is,
    To feel my Saviour mine.

My friends, for you I long,
    That you might happy be;
I long to hear you sing the song,
    Jesus has died for me.

How short and fleeting are my days,
    And chiefly spent in sinful ways;
O may those few which now remain
    Be spent eternal life to gain.

I'm passing through this vale of tears
    Beneath the weight of numerous years,
My body maimed; what have I done
    Beneath the light of yonder sun.

The bloom of life I spent in vain
    Some earthly treasures to obtain;
But earthly treasures took their flight,
    For which I laboured day and night.

I've ranged the fields of battle o'er
    Midst dying groans and cannon's roar;
Whilst death surrounded all the plain,
    I'm spared amidst the thousands slain.

I've been preserved by sea and land
By the Almighty's gracious hand,
For causes then unknown to me,
Which since I trust I'm brought to see.

I hope through grace that God has given
I'm led to seek a place in heaven;
Where sin and pain shall never come,
I hope to find a peaceful home.

GRANDSONS OF SOLOMON MACK, CHILION MACK (LEFT) AND SOLOMON MACK III (right).

CHAPTER 4

Lovisa Mack's Healing

Solomon Mack added the noteworthy healing of his daughter Lovisa at the end of his *Narrative*. Not strictly pertinent to his autobiography, it remarkably illustrates the Christian faith of his home when he was middle-aged. As mentioned, Solomon paid earnest tribute to his wife for schooling their children in "love towards each other, as well as devotional feelings towards him who made them." Such teaching effectively motivated all their children, and intensely the daughters, the youngest of which was Lucy, the mother of Joseph Smith, Jr. She also made a record of the interrelated deaths of her sisters, Lovisa Mack Tuttle and Lovina Mack.

The personalities of Solomon and his daughter Lucy come alive in their individual accounts of Lovisa's last days. As elsewhere in her history, Lucy is photographic in detail, but Solomon underplays the event. With skepticism, one could say that Lucy adorns the incident with dramatic license, but that is not likely. The sudden healing was miraculous, and even Solomon says that it was preceded by a prophetic dream, details of which are obviously lacking in his spare summary. Moreover, careful research has shown Lucy to be highly accurate in her names and episodes of New England and western New York.[95] Her greater detail simply shows her talent for graphic narrative, and reflects intimacy with Lovisa in visits in the Mack and Tuttle homes, when these sisters shared close companionship. Thus Solomon Mack's writing is far short of exaggeration, factual to the fault of terseness. He evidently would not overstate his own exploits or spiritual experiences.

Without contrivance it is nearly impossible for two observers to tell an identical story. In outline Lucy and her father agree completely; in most details they supplement each other—occasionally discrepancies appear, proving independent information or recollection. As a sister Lucy would obviously pay more attention to particulars of the sickness. In the case of the proprietor of the Montague inn where Lovisa died, Solomon remembered the name as beginning with "S", whereas Lucy is specific on "Taff." Solomon was there, and Lucy was not; yet she committed an accurate error, for in 1794 one innkeeper was Severance and another Taft. The two inns were about two miles apart, both probably run by friends of Solomon, since he had lived years in Montague before that.[96] Possibly he mentioned both individuals as helping him in the personal tragedy of his daughter's dying on her journey home. By contrast Lucy Smith seems more concerned with time than her father and is likely to be more accurate in her estimates, with one qualification. Whereas Solomon's terse record sets no date, the daughter measures events from the marriage of her oldest sister, an event of 1780, when Lucy was but four.[97] One cannot demand precision so early, but Lucy's dates work back well from her own marriage, and her memory is demonstrably accurate in mid-adolescence.

Two youthful recollections of Lucy Smith prove this point. Her preliminary manuscript mentions birth in New Hampshire and moving to western Massachusetts:

> From Gilsum father moved to Montague. Here I became acquainted with the family of Captain Gun: Thankful, Unice, Abel, and Martin—also the Harvys' children. I mention these as I shall also others as I pass along in hopes that this may reach them, and by this means I shall be able to make myself known to them.

Lucy was about four when her father first moved to Montague, around 1779, and the Macks remained in that vicinity until Lucy was about thirteen. Her friends all appear in Montague records. Two Harvey families had children who were likely her playmates, and the birth years of the Gunn children are as follows: Thankful, 1754; Eunice, 1762; Abel, 1766; Martin, 1769. These children ranged from ten to twenty-five when Lucy moved there as a child. And their father Asahel is titled "Capt." on his gravestone, exactly as Lucy refers to him.[98] Her memory of early personal relationships is excellent.

A second recollection concerns Lucy's adolescent visit to her married sister, an immediate continuation of the indented quotation above:

> Two years before sister Lovina's death I visited sister Tuttle, who was then sick at South Hadley. Here lived one Colonel Woodbridge, who bought a large church bell about this time, which was hung while I was there, and I understand remains till this day. A company of young folks went to see it when it was first hung. I was one of the number and was the first who ever rang the bell. This Colonel W[oodbridge] afterwards built a large establishment for the education of poor children. Before I returned home my father moved back to Gilsum, where I continued with my parents until my youngest sister's death.

Lucy gives the right name, title, and locality for "Ruggles Woodbridge, Esqr.," as he is called in the 1790 census at South Hadley. He is titled "Colonel" in the town records and by the early historian Judd, who claimed that Woodbridge had "commanded a regiment in the Revolutionary War."[99] As Lucy indicates, this well-to-do philanthropist operated a school,[100] but his donation of the bell rung by Lucy furnishes a firm date in her life. In 1791 the town voted thanks "to Col. R. Woodbridge for his liberal offer to them respecting his giving a bell to the town." That year the town agreed to build a steeple and belfry, which were evidently finished by June 18, 1792; a "second recasting" of the cracked bell in the following year proves that Lucy visited Lovisa ("when it was first hung") in 1791-92.[101] Although Lucy recalled these events a half century later, she constantly impresses the local historian, who rates her good to precise in ability to furnish specific facts.

The bell episode is crucial in Lovisa's story, for she would be alive in 1792, though "then sick." Memory from a surprising source confirms this picture. Solomon Mack says that his daughter married Joseph Tuttle, an event of early 1780 in town records.[102] After Lovisa died, Joseph (1756-1816) remarried, and his eldest son Joseph (1796-1884) was unschooled but a successful farmer with an alert mind. He wrote with unusual detail about his grandfather John Tuttle and father Joseph Tuttle, who died when the younger Joseph was twenty and well aware of the earlier life of his father.[103] His reference to "Capt. Mack" has already been quoted, but Tuttle also described Lovisa:

> My father was twice married. His first wife was Lovice Mack, a daughter of old Capt. Mack, of Sunderland, Mass. Her father was an old sea captain and was well known in that vicinity. Another of his daughters married Joseph Smith and became the mother of the celebrated Mormon Prophet of the same name. By his first wife my father raised no children, she being an invalid most of her life, and dying childless, fourteen years after her marriage.[104]

This indicates 1794 as the year of the death of Lovisa —and also the interrelated death of her younger sister Lovina.[105] The chronology chart on pages 68-69 simplifies these events and shows how Lucy Smith's recollections fit both the bell episode and the Joseph Tuttle history. The deaths of her sisters have sometimes been set at 1788, based on one of Lucy's statements;[106] however, her total writings give a different result.[107] Lucy remembers the following time sequence for Lovisa: marriage, two years of health, two years of sickness before healing, and three final years of life. Adding these intervals to Lovisa's marriage (1780) is not satisfactory either in result or the method of trusting Lucy's measure-

ments in early childhood. But when one works the same
intervals back from Lovisa's death (1794), a surprising
coincidence appears. Lucy's chronology ties into sister
Lydia's marriage. The wedding festivity when she was
four could easily have been confused with the similar
celebration when she was ten. This appears to be an
error of some logic, a wedding correctly remembered but
two sisters confused because of Lucy's early age.

Documents regarding Lovisa mention Montague,
Sunderland, Hadley, and South Hadley, all adjoining
towns of western Massachusetts on a north-south line
from each other. Lovisa was married in Montague, where
her father's family appears on the 1790 census.[108] Some
two years later (as discussed in his biography), Solomon
Mack moved back to Gilsum, New Hampshire, from
which he later made his sixty-mile trip to bring Lovisa
home in her last sickness (1794). Lucy remembers her
then at South Hadley, where Lucy had visited her two
years earlier.[109] But in 1790 Joseph Tuttle is enumerated
in Hadley, with one male and two females in the household. Lovisa was childless, so the second female is possibly Lovina, who nursed her older sister some two
years.[110] Despite Lovisa's residence in South Hadley-
Hadley, her healing (Solomon says) took place in Sunderland, where Lovisa afterward walked across the street to
her father-in-law's. In 1790 John Tuttle lived in Sunderland.[111] Furthermore, the Tuttle tradition fixed that as a
continuous residence where his sons lived about him:

> When my father was three years old, my grandfather removed
> from Lebanon, Conn., to Sunderland, Mass., where he afterwards
> died. He was lifting a stick of timber with another man, who threw
> down his end, which jarred grandfather and broke a blood vessel.
> . . . My grandfather's name was John, and he was also a mechanic,
> having the trades of wheelwright, carpenter, and stone mason. . . .
> My grandfather Tuttle was a soldier in the old French and Indian
> War. He died with his son, in Sunderland, Mass. I have heard my
> father relate that according to the custom of the times, he and his
> brother John presented the remains of their father at the door of
> the house for burial.[112]

A CHRONOLOGY FOR THE MACK SISTERS

This list of dates summarizes events surrounding Lovisa Mack's death, as explained in the introduction to this chapter. Estimates carry *c.*, abbreviation for Latin *circa*, "about." Lucy Smith's preliminary manuscript and published *Biographical Sketches* are given without author. Her memory of relationships is nearly exact for events after adolescence. This is checked by the definite dates of the bell episode, her own marriage, and the Joseph Tuttle manuscript.

Date	*Event*	*Evidence for Dating*
1759 (Jan. 4)	Solomon's Marriage	Vital Records, Lyme, Conn.
c. 1761	Lovisa's Birth	"My oldest sister's faith" (preliminary ms.).
c. 1762	Lovina's Birth	"My youngest sister's death" (preliminary ms.).
c. 1764	Lydia's Birth	Gravestone inscription (see n. 86).
1775 (July 8)	Lucy's Birth	Vital Records, Gilsum, N. H.
1780 (Jan. 31)	Lovisa's Marriage	Vital Records, Montague, Mass.
1786 (Jan. 26)	Lydia's Marriage	Vital Records, Gilsum, N. H.
c. 1789	Lovisa's Early Sickness	"Her illness lasted two years" (*Biographical Sketches;* preliminary ms. agrees); "about one year" (Solomon Mack, *Narrative*).
c. 1791	Lovisa's Healing	See four entries following.
1792	Lucy's Visit to Lovisa	"Two years before sister Lovina's death I visited sister Tuttle, who was then sick. . . . [A] large church bell . . . was hung while I was there" (preliminary ms.).

1792	Bell Hanging	Money then appropriated for belfry at South Hadley (Town Record Book).
1794	Lovina's Death	Sickness "a short time" before Lovisa's healing, with "three years" affliction (*Biographical Sketches* and preliminary ms.).
1794	Lovisa's Death	Lovisa died "a few months" after Lovina's death (*Biographical Sketches*); "fourteen years after her marriage" ("Narrative . . . of Joseph Tuttle").
1794-95	Lucy's First Tunbridge Stay	"Shortly after" Lovina's death, Lucy went to Stephen Mack's and stayed one year (*Biographical Sketches* and preliminary ms.).
1795	Lucy's Gilsum Return	Lucy "was home but a short time" before returning to Tunbridge, where she was married "the next January" (*Biographical Sketches;* preliminary ms. agrees).
1796 (Jan. 24)	Lucy's Marriage	Vital Records, Tunbridge, Vt.

Lovisa might be near John Tuttle at her healing about 1791 at Sunderland, though she was at Hadley in 1790 (census), and South Hadley in 1792 and in 1794 (Lucy's recollections). She and Joseph Tuttle were childless and could easily move. Her needs evidently forced the husband to bring his critically ill wife near his father's household. Upon Lovisa's recovery perhaps she and Joseph moved to South Hadley, where Lucy visited them. Another possibility is that Lucy remembered the social activity of neighboring South Hadley, though the Tuttles' actual residence may have been Hadley.

Lucy's story about Lovisa is compelling narrative, but is somewhat diminished in parallel study. The harmony also artificially shortens the drama of Lovina's similar illness, though that is available in Lucy Smith's published history. Yet parallel presentation is an excellent tool for understanding all the events that Solomon briefly summarizes, since it adds Lucy Smith's preliminary version and her more polished account, plus historical information integrating with family recollections. For purposes of comparison, minor liberties are taken with the order of Lucy's two narratives, though the sequence of Solomon's brief account is unmodified. Generally there is little difference between Lucy's preliminary manuscript and the 1853 printing, though early personal details were sometimes passed over in revision. For instance, only Lucy's preliminary manuscript mentions the relative ages of Lovisa and Lovina, incidental to beginning their record: "Lovisa, my oldest sister, was a woman [of] peculiar faith, as well as . . . her sister next to her, Lovina." This defines what Lucy means by her inexact reference to Lovina as her "youngest sister" (n. 105). Everything that Solomon and Lucy narrate about Lovisa is included in the following presentation, with the exception of the preliminary manuscript's closing lines of Lovisa's final poem: "Farewell, farewell; in heaven I shall I hope in to meet you all." The line is not completely coherent with itself or the preceding lines. The poetry at the end of Lucy's two accounts is obviously interrelated, but not necessarily two versions of the same poem. According to Lucy's strict language, one was composed "a few days previous" to Lovisa's death, while the broken lines were made "just before she started" for Gilsum the day of her death.

These details introduce the family history of Lovisa's healing.[113] What is its significance? Although belief in miracles is superstition to some, the spectacular change in this dying woman requires serious reflection. Her vision preceded a supernatural recovery; she also made constructive use of the experience—encouraging others to

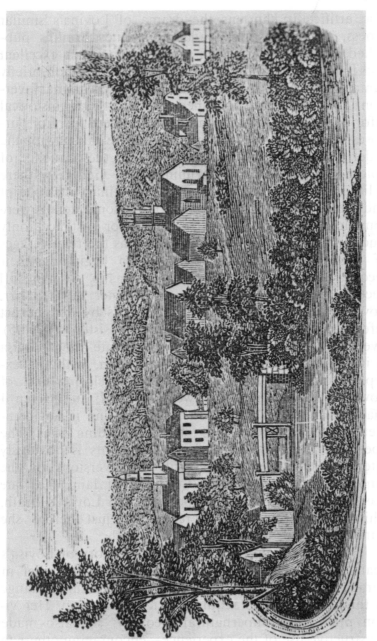

MONTAGUE, MASSACHUSETTS, ABOUT 1838

a better life and drawing attention to God, not herself. Her profound faith is reflected in the psalms she sang in church, no doubt in the versification popularly used in New England. Watts' psalmody was then standard and was divided into the sections cited in Solomon Mack's *Narrative*. Sample stanzas sung publicly by Lovisa disclose her inner feelings then:

> I love the Lord: he heard my cries
> And pity'd every groan.
> Long as I live, when troubles rise,
> I'll hasten to his throne.
>
> The Lord beheld me sore distress't;
> He bid my pains remove.
> Return, my soul, to God thy rest,
> For thou hast known his love.[114]

Both father and sister justly viewed Lovisa as a model of Christian piety, rewarded for her faith by the revelation and intervention of God. Evidently the majority of her friends and neighbors agreed. This raises basic questions about the early revelations of Joseph Smith. Genuine spirituality is a family characteristic. Their sincerity throws great doubt on any theory of deception by him.

THE HEALING
OF LOVISA MACK TUTTLE

Lucy Smith, *Biographical Sketches*   Solomon Mack, *Narrative*

The history of Lovisa and Lovina, my two oldest sisters, is so connected and interwoven that I shall not attempt to separate it. They were one in faith, in love, in action, and in hope of eternal life. They were always together, and when they were old enough to understand the duties of a Christian, they united their voices in prayer and songs of praise to God. This sisterly affection increased with their years, and strengthened with the strength of their minds. The pathway of their lives was never clouded with a gloomy shadow until Lovisa's marriage and removal from home, which left Lovina very lonely.

Quite a miracle of my daughter, in the town of Sunderland, in the state of Massachusetts, the wife of Joseph Tuttle.

I shall here relate a circumstance connected with her sickness, which may try the credulity of some of my readers. Yet hundreds were eye witnesses, and doubtless many of them are now living, who, if they would, could testify to the fact which I am about to mention.

In about two years after Lovisa's marriage she was taken very sick, and sent for Lovina. Lovina, as might be expected, went immediately, and remained with her sister during her illness, which lasted two years, baffling the skill of the most experienced physicians. But at the expiration of this time she revived a little, and showed some symptoms of recovery.

She was sick about one year. At the expiration of her first sickness, the doctor had given her over, and the nurses removed her by the use of sheets to make her bed for some days before her recovery.

Historical Correlations   Lucy Smith, Preliminary Manuscript

Vital Records of Montague, Massachusetts (Salem, Mass., 1934), "Montague Marriages," p. 91: "Lovisa Mack and Joseph Tuttle, Jan. 31, 1780."

Lovisa, my oldest sister, was a woman [of] peculiar faith, as well as my oldest brother and her sister next to her, Lovina. These two were singular for their devoted attachment for each other, which continued steadfast till death. And of their death one might well say as did one of old, let me die the death of the righteous and let my last end be like theirs. I shall not weary my reader with recitals of early life, which though they are engraved upon my heart with a pen of iron, never to be obliterated, might not touch the feelings of others with that interest with which I contemplate the same.

I shall here relate a circumstance that may tax the credulity of such as do not bear witness of the fact as I do —who are not a few. But what I say here I say with reference to eternity and the judgment seat of the Almighty, where I shall again meet my readers as a testator of the same.

"My father was twice married. His first wife was Lovice Mack . . . , she being an invalid most of her life." "Narrative of . . . Joseph Tuttle."

But to my tale. An example of my oldest sister's faith, which I shall here give, was exhibited years subsequent to her marriage. She was taken violently sick with a disease so singular in its nature that her attendant physicians not being furnished with any precedent, could give no name to. Suffice it to say, she was nigh unto death and sorely afflicted for the space of two years. She revived a little about this time and showed some symptoms of recovery.

Lucy Smith, *Biographical Sketches*   Solomon Mack, *Narrative*

As before stated, after the space of two years she began to manifest signs of convalescence, but soon a violent reattack brought her down again, and she grew worse and worse, until she became entirely speechless and so reduced that her attendants were not allowed to even turn her in bed. She took no nourishment except a very little rice water. She lay in this situation three days and two nights.

For three days she [ate] only the yoke of one egg—she was an anatomy to appearance. Her friends were often weeping around her bed, expecting every moment to be her last. The day before her recovery, the doctor said it was as much impossible to raise her, as it would one from the dead.

On the third night, about two o'clock, she feebly pronounced the name of Lovina, who had all the while watched over her pillow like an attendant angel, observing every change and symptom with the deepest emotion. Startled at hearing the sound of Lovisa's voice, Lovina now bent over the emaciated form of her sister with thrilling interest and said, "My sister! My sister! What will you?" Lovisa then said emphatically, "The Lord has healed me, both soul and body—raise me up and give me my clothes; I wish to get up." Her husband told those who were watching with her to gratify her, as in all probability it was a revival before death, and he would not have her crossed in her last moments. They did so, though with reluctance, as they supposed she might live a few moments longer if she did not exhaust her strength too much by exerting herself in this manner. Having raised her in bed, they assisted her to dress. And although when they raised her to her feet, her weight dis-

The night following she dreamed a dream; it was that a sort of wine would cure her. It was immediately brought to her, and she drank it. The next morning she awoke and called to her husband to get up and make a fire. He arose immediately, but thought she was out of her head. But soon he found to the contrary. Quickly she arose up on end in the bed, said the Lord has helped both body and soul, and dressed herself. She then asked for the Psalm Book and turned to the 30th Psalm, second part (readers look for yourselves), and again she mentioned the 116th, first part.

Historical Correlations

Lucy Smith, Preliminary Manuscript

But a malignant reattack soon brought her back in intense agony upon a bed of pain and languor. She grew worse and worse until she became utterly speechless, and was so for several days. Those who attended her were not allowed to move her. She ate not; she drank not, with the exception of a mere morsel of rice water, which they were enabled to pour into her mouth with a teaspoon by prying her teeth apart.

1790 Census, Hadley, Massachusetts: Joseph Tuttle household enumerated with 1 male over 16 and 2 females.

Thus she lay until the night of the third day at about two o'clock. She feebly pronounced the name of her sister Lovina, who had hovered indefatigably all the while around her pillow night and day like an attendant angel, watching every change with thrilling anxiety. She now bent with deep emotion over the emaciated form of the invalid and said, "My sister!" —but no more; her feelings choked her utterance. Lovisa said emphatically, "The Lord has healed me, soul and body—raise me up, and give me my clothes. I want to get up." Her husband told those present to gratify her, as this was probably a revival before death, and he would not have her crossed in her last moments. They raised her in bed and handed her clothing to her and assisted her to dress. But when she was lifted to her feet, both of her ankles were instantly dislocated by her weight resting upon them. She said, "Put me in a chair and pull my feet gently, and I shall soon be sound again." She then ordered

Lucy Smith, *Biographical Sketches*   Solomon Mack, *Narrative*

located both of her ankles, she would
not consent to return to her bed, but
insisted upon being set in a chair
and having her feet drawn gently in
order to have her ankle joints replaced.
She then requested her husband to
bring her some wine, saying if he
would do so, she would do quite well
for the present.

Soon after this, by her own request she was assisted to cross the
street to her father-in-law's, who was
at that time prostrated upon a bed of
sickness. When she entered the house
he cried out in amazement, "Lovisa is
dead, and her spirit is now come to
warn me of my sudden departure from
this world." "No, father," she exclaimed, "God has raised me up, and
I have come to tell you to prepare for
death." She conversed an hour or so
with him; then, with the assistance of
her husband and those who attended
upon her that night, she crossed the
street back again to her own apart-
ment.

Soon after, the same
morning, she went to the
house of her father-in-law
(which was about ten rods)
and back again on her feet.
Her eyes and countenance
appeared lively and bright
as ever it was in her past
life.

When this was noised abroad a
great multitude of people came
together, both to hear and see concerning the strange and marvelous
circumstance which had taken place.
She talked to them a short time and
then sang a hymn, after which she dis-
missed them, promising to meet them
the next day at the village church,
where she would tell them all about
the strange manner in which she had
been healed.

Historical Correlations	Lucy Smith, Preliminary Manuscript

her husband to bring her nourishment.

"My grandfather Tuttle . . . died with his son, in Sunderland, Massachusetts." Narrative of . . . Joseph Tuttle."

1790 census, Sunderland, Massachusetts, enumerates John Tuttle and household.

When she had taken some stimulance she desired them to assist her to cross the street to her father-in-law's, who was then sick. They did so. When she entered, he cried out in amazement, "Lovisa is dead, and her spirit has come to admonish me of my final exit." "No, father, no," she said; "God has raised me up, and I come to tell you to prepare for death." She then sat down, conversed with him some time, and afterwards returned home by this help of her husband and three watchers that had been sitting up with her—for she had not been without two extra attendants one night for one whole year.

By this time so great an excitement was raised that the inhabitants began to gather from all quarters. She told them she would meet them at the village church on Thursday, the next day, and tell them all they wished to know,

Lucy Smith, *Biographical Sketches*   Solomon Mack, *Narrative*

The following day, acording to promise, she proceeded to the church, and when she arrived there a large congregation had collected. Soon after she entered, the minister arose and remarked that as many of the congregation had doubtless come to hear a recital of the strange circumstance which had taken place in the neighborhood, and as he himself felt more interested in it than in hearing a gospel discourse, he would open the meeting and then give place to Mrs. Tuttle.

It was on Thursday following, she went to meeting, which was a mile and a half.

The minister then requested her to sing a hymn. She accordingly did so, and her voice was as high and clear as it had ever been. Having sung, she arose and addressed the audience as follows: "I seemed to be borne away to the world of spirits, where I saw the Savior, as through a veil, which appeared to me about as thick as a spider's web. And he told me that I must return again to warn the people to prepare for death; that I must exhort them to be watchful as well as prayerful; that I must declare faithfully unto them their accountability before God, and the certainty of their being called to stand before the judgment seat of Christ; and that if I would do this, my life should be prolonged." After which she spoke much to the people upon the uncertainty of life. When she sat down her husband and sister, also those who were with her during the last night of her sickness, arose and testified to her appearance just before her sudden recovery.

On the first singing she offered them the 116th Psalm, first part. The minister preached an excellent sermon, but her exhortation was said to exceed the minister's sermon, and on the last singing she turned to the 116th Psalm, second part.

Historical Correlations

Lucy Smith, Preliminary Manuscript

which she accordingly did by walking one mile with the assistance of her husband and her sister. [The] minister opened the meeting and gave it into her hands.

Stanza of the Watts' 116th Psalm:

My God hath sav'd my soul from death

And dry'd my falling tears.

Now to his praise I'll spend my breath,

And my remaining years.

She then sang them a hymn with angelic harmony. She sang a splendid strain of music. She occupied the whole day. [She] had her two nurses with [her]. [She] told them when she lay sick she was carried away. There was nothing more than a spider's web between her and Christ—that Christ bid her return and warn the people. She testified with boldness to the power of God in her behalf and continued so to do till her death, which was three years after.

Lucy Smith, *Biographical Sketches*   Solomon Mack, *Narrative*

Of these things she continued to speak boldly for the space of three years, at the end of which time she was seized with the consumption, which terminated her earthly existence.

After meeting [she] returned home. And after she regained her strength she went about her usual labor, which she moderately followed one or two years, when she was taken down again. She grew uneasy and went to her father's in Gilsum, in New Hampshire, and there stayed some months.

A short time before Lovisa was healed in the miraculous manner before stated, Lovina was taken with a severe cough, which ended in consumption. She lingered three years, during which time she spoke with much calmness of her approaching dissolution, contemplating death with all that serenity which is characteristic of the last moments of those who fear God and walk uprightly before him. She conjured her young friends to remember that life upon this earth cannot be eternal. Hence the necessity of looking beyond this vale of tears to a glorious inheritance, where moths do not corrupt nor thieves break through and steal. . . .

At the same time I had another daughter sick with the consumption, and died.

Having led my readers to the close of Lovina's life, I shall return to Lovisa, of whom there only remains the closing scene of her earthly career. In the course of a few months subsequent to the death of sister Lovina, my father received a letter from South Hadley, stating that Lovisa was very

My other daughter grew uneasy, and I carried her back again, where she staid part of one summer, and she was discontented.

Historical Correlations

Lucy Smith, Preliminary Manuscript

She preached to a crowded house. After this her house was always crowded for three years.

Lovina's character was that of a true follower of Christ, and she lived contemplating her final change with that peaceful serenity which characterizes those who fear God and walk uprightly. She was taken with the consumption at sixteen and languished three years with this fatal disease. She spoke calmly of her approaching dissolution and conjured her young friends to remember that life upon this earth could not be eternal; therefore the necessity of looking beyond this vale of tears to a far more glorious inheritance laid up, where moth doth not corrupt nor thieves break through nor steal. . . .

After she took sick [she] sent for father to come and see her. She was afraid she should die before he got there.

Lucy Smith, *Biographical Sketches*   Solomon   Mack,   *Narrative*

low of the consumption, and that she
earnestly desired him to come and
see her as soon as possible, as she
expected to live but a short time.

My father set out immediately, and   And I went after her,
when he arrived there, he found her
in rather better health than he expected. In a few days after he got
there, she resolved in her heart to
return with him at all hazards. To
this her father unwillingly consented,
and after making the requisite preparations they started for Gilsum.

They traveled about four miles   and got her to Montague to
and came to an inn kept by a man   landlord S_____. I took her
by the name of Taff. Here her father   out of the carriage and set
halted and asked her if she did not   her in a chair, and she in-
wish to tarry a short time to rest her-   stantly died.
self. She replied in the affirmative. By
the assistance of the landlord she was
presently seated in an easy chair. My
father then stepped into the next room
to procure a little water and wine for
her. He was absent but a moment;
however when he returned it was too
late. Her spirit had fled from its
earthly tabernacle to return no more
until recalled by the trump of the
Archangel.

My father immediately addressed   I immediately got a
a letter to mother, informing her of   coffin made and then car-
Lovisa's death, lest the shock of see- ried her home.
ing the corpse unexpectedly should
overcome her. And as soon as he could
get a coffin, he proceeded on his
journey for Gilsum, a distance of fifty

Historical Correlations

Lucy Smith, Preliminary Manuscript

He went in a carriage. She would go back with him. He prepared a bed, laid her thereon. She then told him, "Now, father, if I die before I get home, I wish you to bury me in Gilsum beside my sister Lovina."

1794 map of Montague lists "Taft's Tavern" and "Severance's Tavern" (see discussion). 1790 Census, Montague, Massachusetts, enumerates Lyman Taft and Moses Severance.

[He] traveled four miles, put up at Mr. Taffe's. [He] asked her if she would be placed in a chair and rest a little. She said she would, and after she was taken into the parlor, while father went to the bar for some spirits she expired in her chair.

"By his first wife my father raised no children, she . . . dying childless fourteen years after her marriage." "Narrative of . . . Joseph Tuttle."

Father then did all that could be done by way of decent dress and suitable equipage of every kind. It was fifty miles from there to Gilsum. [He] kept her three days, then buried her as her request was. Father took the precaution of writing to mother—almost

Lucy Smith, *Biographical Sketches*   Solomon Mack, *Narrative*

miles. She was buried by the side of her
sister Lovina, according to her own
request.

The following is part of a hymn
composed by herself a few days previous to her decease:

Lord, may my thoughts be turned
to thee;
Lift thou my heavy soul on high;
Wilt thou, O Lord, return to me
In mercy, Father, ere I die!
My soaring thoughts now rise
above—
Oh, fill my soul with heavenly
love.

Father and mother, now farewell;
And husband, partner of my life,
Go to my father's children, tell
That lives no more on earth thy
wife;
That while she dwelt in cumbrous
clay,
For them she prayed both night
and day.

My friends, I bid you all adieu;
The Lord hath called, and I must
go—
And all the joys of this vain earth
Are now to me of little worth;
Twill be the same with you as me,
When brought as near eternity.

Thus closes this mournful recital.
And when I pass with my readers into
the next chapter, with them probably
may end the sympathy aroused by
this rehearsal—but with me it must
last while life endures.

Historical Correlations Lucy Smith, Preliminary Manuscript

overcome. [He] went fifteen miles for a minister to preach. I was then in Tunbridge with brother S[tephen] Mack.

She made some verses just before she started:

O Lord, wilt thou return to me
In mercy, Lord, before I die.
Oh, may I now return to thee
And lift my heavy soul on high.

Oh, for mercy I implore,
(And never sin no more);
And lift my heavy soul above,
And fill my soul with heavenly love.

Farewell, my father and my mother
    dear,
Farewell, my husband of my life,
Farewell, my brothers and sisters
    here,
And farewell, all the joys of life.

(For whilst with you on earth I
    stay,
I beg your prayers both night and
    day.)

Farewell, oh world, I bid adieu;
The Lord he calls, and I must go.
For I must, and soon be gone—
My time on earth will not be long.

PATERNAL LINE OF JOSEPH SMITH, 1805-1844

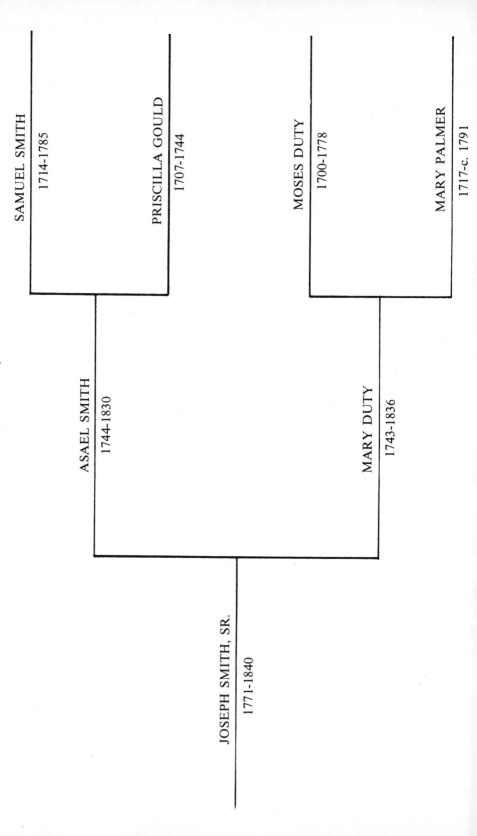

SAMUEL SMITH
1714-1785

PRISCILLA GOULD
1707-1744

MOSES DUTY
1700-1778

MARY PALMER
1717-c. 1791

ASAEL SMITH
1744-1830

MARY DUTY
1743-1836

JOSEPH SMITH, SR.
1771-1840

CHAPTER 5

Lives of Asael and Mary Duty Smith

Asael Smith could look to illustrious Massachusetts ancestry, but just being the youngest child of prominent Samuel Smith was an education in public service.[115] Samuel would be better known had he lived in an urban center, for he repeatedly held the most responsible positions in Topsfield, north of Boston. His record of offices is remarkable: a half-dozen terms in the state legislature, a dozen terms as a governing selectman of his town, and sometime town clerk.[116] The full story of community prominence is too voluminous to mention here.[117] Captain in the militia and a grass-roots leader in committees that successfully promoted the Revolution, Samuel Smith was a solid representative of the local aristocracies that had the most to lose by pledging lives, fortunes, and sacred honor for the cause of American independence.[118] Samuel affirmed his faith in the preamble of his will; though using a common formula, he subscribed to the Christian conviction that by "the mighty power of God" he would stand again at "the general resurrection."[119] A highly religious man who took his Congregational covenant seriously, he was active in public worship. His five children were all baptized in the Topsfield church, including youngest Asael four days after birth.[120]

The various strands of an admirable life are summed up in the father's 1785 obituary:

DIED—At Topsfield, on Monday the 14th instant, Samuel Smith, Esq., aged 72. So amiable and worthy a character as he evidently appeared, both in publick and private, will render the memory of

W. Stockholm
Potsdam

VERMONT

NEW

YORK

NEW
HAMPSHIRE

Tunbridge

Royalton

Merrimack River

Derryfield
(Manchester)

Dunbarton   Rowley

Windham

Ipswich

Topsfield

Salem

Boston

**PLACES IN
ASAEL
SMITH'S
LIFE**

Connecticut River

MASSACHUSETTS

CONN.   R. I.

Known
Residences
Underlined

him ever precious. For a number of years he represented the town in the General Court, where he was esteemed a man of integrity and uprightness. His usefulness among those with whom he was more immediately conversant, was eminent. He was a sincere friend to the liberties of his country, and a strenuous advocate for the doctrines of Christianity. "The memory of the just is blessed."[121]

At his father's passing, Asael Smith was a married man with ten children, living in Derryfield (now Manchester), New Hampshire, where he was serving his seventh term as town clerk. Born in 1744, he had earlier shared the work of his father's farms at Topsfield, Massachusetts.[122] At age nineteen Asael signed as a witness in Samuel's sale of 120 acres on the northern border of Topsfield. His father soon purchased a somewhat smaller acreage a mile or more north of the Topsfield common.[123] On Pye Brook, the farm included "tillage land" and orchard, but was managed more for hay and meadow and the livestock it supported.[124] Asael was only the second son, so economic custom dictated his learning a trade and leaving the family homestead, allowing his older brother, Samuel Smith, Jr., to farm on shares with his father. But life would strangely reverse this situation years later.

When Asael turned twenty-one, he was added to the tax list after "Captain Samuel Smith" and Samuel Smith, Jr.[125] At twenty-three Asael wedded Mary Duty, though the couple continued to live on the family farm during early marriage.[126] Mary also came from a religious family and had been baptized as an infant in the Congregational pattern.[127] Their first three children were born in Topsfield; the third was Joseph, born July 12, 1771, whose birth entry was later annotated in the town records: "This Joseph was father of Joseph the Mormon."[128] The home of Asael and Mary Smith was Christian, witnessed by the baptisms of these children in Topsfield March 8, 1772. On that day the church minutes record their own profession of faith: "Asael Smith and

Mary his wife . . . owned the covenant."[129] Their children of 1773 and 1775 were born in Windham, New Hampshire, Mary's former home.[130] The move to New Hampshire and the stay in nearby communities there were summarized in a bare historical note on the inside cover of a pamphlet:

> Asael Smith, his book. May the first, 1772 we removed from Topsfield and dwelt at Windham in New Hampshire. And April the 15th, 1774 we removed from Windham, and now we dwell at Dunbarton, New Hampshire.[131]

Joseph Smith claimed the "love of liberty" from both grandfathers.[132] While Samuel Smith served in the political councils of the Revolution, his son Asael enlisted as a soldier. In the summer of 1776 he mustered under Captain John Nesmith in "a company raised for Canada service," an act of obvious hardship for a family head with six dependents. His regiment was enrolled to defend New York's northern frontier.[133] Possibly exertion and disease took their toll in 1776—a decade later Asael was "in a low state of health, entirely unable to labor for three years."[134] His heartfelt approval of the American Revolution is clear—at the crest of life he stated his political credo for his family:

> Bless God that you live in a land of liberty, and bear yourselves dutifully and conscionably towards the authority under which you live. See God's providence in the appointment of the Federal Constitution, and hold union and order as a precious jewel.[135]

These convictions were taught to Asael's sons and grandsons (the Prophet clearly included), a process symbolized by the continuation of Asael's trade to Joseph Smith, Sr. From age thirty-four to forty-seven, both New Hampshire and Massachusetts deeds refer to "Asael Smith . . . cooper," which identify him by his craftsmanship at barrel-making.[136] Asael evidently set the precedent for his son Silas, later described as "engaged in

THE COMMON, TOPSFIELD, MASSACHUSETTS

farming during the summer, and in winter he worked at
the cooper trade, making full-bound barrels, his sons
assisting him on the farm and in the shop."[137] Post-
Revolutionary land records prove a local move to Derryfield, the area of Manchester, New Hampshire, where
Asael purchased a 100-acre farm on the Merrimack
River May 27, 1778.[138] There he was most prominent in
civic affairs, elected as Derryfield town clerk from 1779
through 1786, an office that Asael resigned after his
father's death.[139] Seven years on the Merrimack land
saw births of four more children, and Asael personally
recorded the birthdates of most of his large family in
the first Derryfield town book.[140] Here his older sons arrived at early manhood, and he heavily depended on
them in operating his farm. The second was the Prophet's
father, Joseph Smith, Sr.

Asael's father willed him his "silver shoe buckles,"
but Samuel's sterling character was a greater inheritance.
An unusual sense of responsibility looms in John Smith's
history of the death of Asael's father—based on childhood
recollection and later intimacy with his own father, Asael.
These personal details fit squarely into known facts and
constitute a significant episode of moral heroism in Asael
Smith's life. John reminisced:

> My grandfather died when I [was] quite young. I remember
> my father's returning home from Massachusetts, where he had been
> to visit his father in his last sickness. I well remember how melan-
> choly he appeared when he called his children round him and told
> us that our grandfather was dead.[141]

Earlier Asael sat with semi-delirious Samuel, whose
powerful drive to provide asserted itself in imagining
himself able to care for his family. John Smith's account
carries an eloquence of event:

> He jumped out of his bed and said he must go to mill, for my
> family will suffer. My father replied, "I will go to mill; I will take
> care of the family. Dear sir, do go to bed." "Asael said he will take

care of my wife." Says he, "I will." To use my father's own words: "He lay down quietly, knowing that I always did as I agreed, and soon after fell asleep and was gathered to his people. This promise cost me much money and trouble, but I never regretted it. I have done as I promised."[142]

The dramatic tension of this obligation comes from both circumstances and personalities. Partly from extensive public service, Samuel "left his own affairs in a condition very difficult to settle by anyone but himself."[143] Furthermore, Asael (now father of eleven) was himself recovering from economic setbacks and poor health. He was youngest of his own family, and his brother and three sisters were self-sufficient. So his promise concerned Samuel's seventy-one-year-old widow, his stepmother, for his mother died in the year of his birth.[144] Asael confided that his stepmother "did not treat him so kindly as some mothers treat their children."[145] Nevertheless he had a strong sense of honor and shouldered duty as few men would. Asael's son preserved the particulars:

My uncle Samuel, who lived with my grandfather at the time of his death, after finding the condition his estate was in, came to New Hampshire to counsel with my father on the subject. He said it was not possible to pay the debts with the property that was left under the then existing circumstances. My father not being so well acquainted with the state of affairs as his elder brother Samuel, thought that it might be done. "For," said he, "I am not willing that my father, who has done so much business, should have it said of him that he died insolvent." And [he] urged hard to have my uncle go on and settle the business, and he felt that the Lord would prosper him in the undertaking. But my uncle said that he had a large family and but very little property, and he could not undertake such a work without the means to do with.

My father was then in low circumstances, had been in a low state of health, entirely unable to labor for three years, during which time he was only able to keep the town record, as he had held the office of town clerk for many years. He owned a small farm in Derryfield, on Merrimack River, a large and growing family, and in consequence of his late sickness [they were] in very destitute

THE HOME OF SAMUEL AND ASAEL SMITH, TOPSFIELD, MASSACHUSETTS

condition. "Notwithstanding all my embarrassments," said my father, "I will undertake to settle my father's estate and save his name from going down to posterity as an insolvent debtor. . . ." After considerable conversation with my uncle, [they] agreed to change places. Accordingly, my father moved his family to Topsfield, Massachusetts and attend[ed] to the business above mentioned.[146]

Records prove that Asael deeded his New Hampshire farm to his brother Samuel and exchanged places.[147] Prior to the father's death the Massachusetts family estate had been taxed in the names of "Samuel Smith, Esq., and his son Samuel"; afterward Asael is taxed at Topsfield.[148] His promise was kept by mental and physical blisters. He managed about 100 acres, raising hay, livestock, and a variety of minor crops.[149]

Here my father struggled hard for about five years and made out to support his family comfortably. His stepmother was on his hands during this time, who was sometimes rather childish. However, by prudence and industry he had paid some part of his father's debts. . . . [H]is old mother received her third, [and] after supporting a large family with the scanty means which was at his command, he could not pay the old debts which were crowding upon him. People showed no lenity, notwithstanding they knew that if he had not have come forward to pay them, they never could have got one-eighth part of what they [were] now determined to have.[150]

In these years Asael was struggling against impossible odds. He was always industrious and a good manager, but sickness and hard times took away every surplus. Describing coming to Massachusetts in 1786, his son says that Asael "had lost considerable in the downfall of Continental paper," a grim condition that had also affected Samuel's estate. This paper dollar lost value during the Revolution, only to reach its low worth below a cent prior to Samuel's death. The decade after the Revolution saw much else that was "not worth a Continental." Debts incurred by the father during heavy inflation had to be repaid by the son during depression, when falling farm prices decreased the cash value of Asael's labors.[151] At the time he sought to pay off his father's obligations, thousands of debtors in rural Massachusetts supported armed revolution (materializing in Shay's Rebellion) rather than face compulsory collection and foreclosure proceedings.[152] But if a failing economy bequeathed impossibility, Asael was generous with his resources. The widow's right was met (perhaps on her demand) by renting a third of the land for her support, but the stepson voluntarily promised to pay necessities that she lacked.[153] By entering the picture, Asael shouldered the burden of paying the widow plus the creditors; the latter obligation came largely out of his pocket, so he correctly said that honoring his father "cost me much money and trouble." Overall, he traded his own land for Samuel's farm; while running it he devoted excess profits to Samuel's creditors; when sold, he distributed virtually the entire return to settle his father's affairs. He might have walked away and let the creditors divide up the estate, with the widow assured of her dower.[154] Instead, with his own labor he paid off all debts in full, by family tradition a net cost of $700 to him. Asael sold the farm but did not keep the proceeds: "He then paid all the debts . . . against the estate and left himself almost destitute of means to support his family."[155] Five years of labor added little to his pocketbook but much to his moral stature.

But Asael could still laugh in adversity, another quality transmitted to Joseph Smith. The grandfather listed his taxable property in a humorous poem, and it was later recovered "among the scraps found on file" in the town archives:

> To the Selectmen of Topsfield:
>
> I have two polls, the one is poor,
> I have three cows and want five more,
> I have no horse, but fifteen sheep—
> No more than these this year I keep;
> Steers that's two years old, one pair,

Two calves I have, all over hair,
Three heifers two years old I own,
One heifer calf that's poorly grown.
My land is acres eighty-two,
Which search the records, you'll find true.
And this is all I have in store—
I'll thank you if you'll tax no more.[156]

Asael Smith

The author of these lines was a confident member of his community, a fact contradicting dubious tradition of Asael's move from Massachusetts because of hostility after befriending a Quaker.[157] Far from being ostracized in Topsfield, he moved to Vermont secure in the many close associations left behind. There he answered a letter of friendship from young but respected Jacob Towne, Jr., prominent farmer who served constantly as selectman, town clerk, or legislator from 1799 to his death in 1836.[158] Towne had an acute mind and was well read. Asael's letter (reproduced in chapter 6) shows a warm relationship with Jacob Towne's parents and other Topsfield families.[159] Mutual regard is obvious with Dr. John Merriam, a practicing physician of high standards, well educated for his day.[160] Joseph Cree had sent respects to Asael, which were returned with the invitation to "set up his trade" in Vermont. Cree was only a small landholder, since he was a craftsman, reportedly a tailor.[161] Asael also greeted Joseph Dorman, who with Ephraim operated the substantial farm that had adjoined his own in Topsfield.[162] Finally, Asael Smith returned "hearty thanks to Mr. Charles Rogers for his respect shown in writing me a few lines"; Rogers was evidently a day laborer and had perhaps worked on Asael's farm.[163] In his 1796 letter, Asael planned to return to friends and neighbors at Topsfield to "pay you a visit." George A. Smith later talked to oldsters with dim memories that Asael did return "and visited his relatives and acquaintances."[164] He was clearly respected in Topsfield, though the sanctimonious could cluck about his religious independence. Fifteen years after Asael left, one Topsfield investor loaned the Smiths $700 in return for their interest-bearing note.[165]

Asael left Topsfield in early 1791, right after he and his stepmother (the widow Priscilla Smith) are enumerated side by side on the 1790 census. Asael was then a vigorous forty-six, and enterprise filled his mind. Temporarily he leased land at Ipswich "with considerable of a stock of cows," and "moved his family on to his hired farm" in the spring of 1791. But Asael did not intend to remain a renter. He let his competent wife supervise the dairy operation, gave "his boys to understand what they must do," and set off for Vermont with his oldest son, Jesse, in quest of inexpensive (and uncleared) land. Events of the move reveal the warmth of Asael's personality. On returning from Vermont, the father made plans to send the two oldest sons to Vermont and make the new place ready. John remembered: "Jesse [then twenty-three] returned with Joseph, my next oldest brother [then twenty], to Vermont to cut away the timber and make preparation for the family to move on —as they then expected—the next spring." Although Jesse and the future father of the Prophet were obviously self-reliant, Asael was too affectionate to carry out the plan: "My father changed his mind, as he could not bear to have his boys so far from him, as he always loved to have his children close by."[166] A personal episode of the move gives another glimpse of Asael's ready wit. Grandson George A. Smith got the story from his father John:

My grandfather had paid a Mr. Averell for making a chest, which it seems Averell was a long time completing, causing a little impatience. At last, however, it was finished. My father said he was walking behind the cart in which they moved into the new state with his father, who on noticing the name of Elijah Averell painted on the box, exclaimed, "In seventeen hundred and ninety-one, Elijah Averell got it done."[167]

50243

For a century memory preserved accurately this moving date, proved by the county and town records of two states and Asael's 1796 letter from Vermont.[168]

The Asael Smiths were hardy pioneers. Their journey from Massachusetts to Vermont is best told in John's memories about the labors of his father and older brothers:

> He sold his crops on the ground and settled his affairs, and set off with family for the new state in the month of October, a journey of 140 miles, thought to be in those days a monstrous long tour. . . . It is through a new country and the roads very bad, the loads heavy. Of course [we] got along very slow—[were] on the road I think 14 days passing through New Hampshire, my native state. . . . During the time we were on the road, but little transpired worthy of note. My brother Asael drove my father's team. He had hired a man by the name of Webster with three yoke of oxen and wagon.
>
> The second or third day we meet with my brother Joseph, who by some accident had partly fractured the bone of his leg and was on the way home, expecting the family to stay at Ipswich through the approaching winter. However, he turned back with us to Vermont. Here my father took his family, went into the woods some distance from any settlement, cut his road and made bridges, and came to the little cabin that my brothers had built for their own accomodation while to work on the land. It was loosely built after the mode of building log huts, say 14 feet by 10. The covering was the bark of the elm, which was very plenty in that part.[169]

Thus "Asael Smith of Ipswich, in the province of Massachusetts Bay," came to Vermont, the deed so decribing him also confirming 1791 as the year Asael took title to eighty-three acres lying in the "Tunbridge gore."[170] Although prominent and successful in his two decades in Tunbridge, he did not lose perspective on the meaning of life. After four years of pioneering in Vermont, he expressed pleasure in both his increasing property and also the close-knit family around him, in a letter to a Topsfield friend:

> My family is all, through the goodness of the divine benediction, in a tolerable good state of health. . . . I have set me up a new

Lincoln Christian College

house . . . and expect to remove into it next spring and to begin again on an entire new farm. And my son Joseph will live on the old farm (if this that has been but four years occupied can be called old) . . . whilst I with my four youngest sons shall endeavor to bring to another farm, etc.[171]

This is also the picture of the Tunbridge records. In 1794 and 1795, more farms of about 100 acres each were purchased by Asael, and further conveyances hint at partnerships with his sons.[172] The oldest son had been married soon after arrival in Vermont, and he owned adjoining property.[173]

The Smiths soon became substantial townsmen of Tunbridge. In 1799 the town clerk noted the creation of a new school district (No. 13) made of "the inhabitants in the neighborhood of Jesse, Joseph and Asael Smith's Jr."[174] Asael, Sr., was at the peak of his powers during his first decade in Tunbridge and became a respected community leader. During 1793 through 1795 he was selectman, one of three elected to manage town affairs. He was on occasion moderator of the town meeting, member of important public committees, highway surveyor in his neighborhood, and grand and petit juror. These were all elective offices that show the trust of his neighbors, and their continuity from 1793 to 1802 is clear evidence of Asael Smith's capacity as a person.[175] Also mentioned in town affairs, his sons continued the tradition of public service.

In this period eligible Lucy Mack was living with her able brother Stephen. Prominent in Tunbridge (as later in Detroit) for his extensive farming and business operations, Stephen Mack is an impressive individual. His friendship with Asael Smith resulted in Lucy's marriage to Asael's son. The Prophet's mother later turned the clock back to Asael Smith's standing in Tunbridge about 1794:

My brother frequently spoke to me of one Mr. Asael Smith, an intimate acquaintance of his, . . . a worthy, respectable, amiable, and intelligent family.[176]

AREA OF ASAEL SMITH'S FARMS, TUNBRIDGE, VERMONT

Asael's personality profile can be accurately reconstructed from his writings. He possessed an admirable New England combination of self-reliance and sense of his own limitations. In his active Tunbridge years he told a Topsfield friend, "I have taken up with the eleventh commandment," referring to an anecdote inventing an additional injunction: "mind your own business." And Asael drew his personal moral: "So I choose to do, and give myself but little concerns about what passes in the political world."[177] No excuse for withdrawal from community leadership, this was an expression of humility about national affairs. There is continuity of this motto through three generations, since the Prophet's brother published it in 1842 as the "Mormon Creed."[178]

Minding one's own business included genuine concern for fellowmen. One of Asael's valued possessions was a pamphlet denouncing the slave trade, given personally to his grandson George A. Smith. "Asael Smith, his hand," several times attested family information entered in the booklet like a treasured family Bible. Grandson George A. observed: "The care with which he preserved this pamphlet and transmitted it to me, makes me think he was a strong anti-slavery man."[179] This work was Benezet's indignant attack on African enslavement, *A Caution and Warning to Great Britain and Her Colonies.* Starting with a premise dear to Asael, the tract insisted that liberty was equally the right of all continents and all races:

> At a time when the general rights and liberties of mankind . . . are become so much the subjects of universal consideration . . . how many . . . advocates of liberty remain insensible and inattentive to the treatment of thousands and tens of thousands of our fellowmen, who from motives of avarice and the inexorable decree of tyrant custom, are at this very time kept in the most deplorable state of slavery in many parts of the British Dominions.[180]

Asael's letter to Topsfield shows how specifically he agreed with these views. His own "little stock of knowledge" was nothing compared to the wisdom of "the Supreme Ruler of universal nature," whose controversy was only beginning with political or clerical oppressors:

He has conducted us through a glorious revolution and has brought us into the promised land of peace and liberty. And I believe that he is about to bring all the world into the same beatitude in his own time and way, which, altho his ways may appear [ever] so inconsistent to our blind reason, yet may be perfectly consistent with his designs. And I believe that the stone is now cut out of the mountain without hands, spoken of by Daniel, and has smitten the image upon his feet, by which . . . all monarchial and ecclesiastical tyranny will be broken to pieces . . . that there shall be no place found for them.[181]

Did God inspire liberty in this life only to enslave men perpetually in the hereafter? Joseph Smith's grandfather resolutely opposed an eternal hell. Such dissenting opinions earned the Topsfield memory that his opinions were more crooked than his neck, a sarcastic reference probably to a damaged tendon.[182] But the comment is more quotable than accurate. Asael was a pewholder in Topsfield—and as Christian as his critics. Whatever Asael's physical flaw, astute grandson George A. Smith knew a well-informed and committed individual:

I remember him as an exceedingly intelligent and cheerful old gentleman with his neck awry, too liberal in his views to please his children, who were convenanters, Congregationalists and Presbyterians, with I think the single exception of his son Joseph [Sr.]. Not long before his death he wrote many quires of paper on the doctrine of universal restoration.[183]

Asael advocated the basic belief of the Universalists of his day, expressed formally by an 1803 New Hampshire convention:

We believe there is one God, whose nature is love, revealed in one Lord Jesus Christ, by one Holy Spirit of grace, who will finally restore the whole family of mankind to holiness and happiness.[184]

Six years before that declaration, a Universalist society was formed in Tunbridge, Vermont, and its members filed formal notice of exemption from "any tax towards the support of any teacher of any different denomination whatever," a reference to the normal town tax for Congregational worship. The moderator of this meeting was Asael Smith, and three of sixteen signers were Asael Smith, together with Jesse and Joseph Smith, his oldest sons.[185]

Universalism sees God as more loving than punishing, and a warm faith in God's personal concern radiates from Asael Smith's most remarkable writing. After his oldest children had married, Asael penned his operating convictions in the form of a will to his family, addressing them in the quaint but endearing term "My Dear Selfs." His "few words of advice" were written and signed April 10, 1799, "for my dearly beloved wife and children to view after my decease."[186] Asael's mature convictions merit careful examination because they throw great light on the personalities of Joseph Smith, Sr., and his son and namesake, Joseph Smith, Jr. This reality of human environment coincided with the wish of the grandfather-testator, who bequeathed to his family "everything that I have in this world but my faults, and them I take with me to the grave . . . leaving my virtues, if ever I had any, to revive and live in you."

Solomon Mack and Asael Smith may have differed on the "universal principle," but they agreed profoundly on the providence of God and the atoning power of the Savior.[187] No responsible biographer can call Asael irreligious, for he held deeply personal convictions about God. "Put your whole trust solely in him," he counseled his wife: "He never did nor never will forsake any that trusted in him." To his children he stressed daily reverence:

Do all to God in a serious manner. When you think of him, speak of him, pray to him, or in any way make your addresses to his great majesty, be in good earnest. Trifle not with his name nor with his attributes, nor call him to witness to anything but is absolute truth.

If Asael were not doctrinally orthodox, the orthodox of his day were often near-sighted Christians. His records in the family Bible show that he honored it, and his quotations prove that he read and believed it. Saturated with passages on Christ's mission, Asael wrote to "pour out my heart" in witness that "the soul is immortal" and that all "stand in need of a Savior," who, in the words of Asael's text, is the "mediator between God and men," giving himself "a ransom for all" (1 Timothy 2:5-6). In fact, Asael devoted about one-fifth of his "will" to scriptural proof that no salvation comes through self-righteousness, but that "sinners must be saved by the righteousness of Christ alone."

Since Asael felt that no amount of "outward forms, rites, and ordinances" could substitute for the experience of Christ's love, he did not point out a "particular form" of religion to his children. But he did counsel them to try every doctrine by tested methods: "admit no others as evidences but the two that God hath appointed, viz., scripture and sound reason." His practical morality stemmed from his relationship with God as a father: "his love is ten thousand times greater towards you than ever any earthly father's could [be] to his offspring." If the author of such views was criticized for his theology, the depth of his Christian devotion is beyond question. Moreover, he promoted organized worship, urging that his family show "honor, obedience, and respect" to the "Church of Christ," the common name then for the Congregational society.

Asael's "will" reveals a man of practiced integrity and unswerving honesty in his thinking about himself. Undoubtedly mirroring his own life, he rated action above words and satisfaction of "your own consciences" above popularity: "[D]o the thing, and do it in a way

that is fair and honest, which you can live and die by
and rise and reign by." If honesty was Asael's guide,
industry was a form of being honest. Perseverance would
succeed in ordinary or eternal affairs. His main enemies
had been "discouragement and unbelief" in his own
abilities. Yet Asael Smith met life's challenges with firm
resolve and effective action—and lost none of his idealism in adversity. He knew self-pity as the opposite of
faith and generosity: "But above everything avoid a melancholy disposition. . . . Shun as death this humor, which
will work you to all unthankfulness against God, unlovingness to men, and unnaturalness to yourselves and one
another."

A profoundly affectionate man, Asael spelled out a
program for family unity after he was gone, leaving his
"last request and charge . . . that you will live together
in an undivided bond of love." This included both personal and economic relationships, since the resources of
all could insure that any "need not want anything." Asael
had practiced a plan of sharing his land with his sons.
Yet individuality was encouraged in his family. Following his creed of minding one's own business, he advised
simply that a vocation should follow one's abilities: "Any
honest calling will honor you if you honor that." Many
a parent has sought to manipulate the right match for
his child, but wise Asael was beyond that:

> As to Your Marriages: I do not think it worthwhile to say much
> about them, for I believe God hath created the persons for each
> other and that nature will find its own.[188]

Asael had earlier "found his own" in Mary Duty
Smith, whom he addressed as "my dearly beloved wife"
after thirty years of marriage.[189] If her biography is fine-
spun, her husband tells what kind of home environment
she created. The Family Address significantly begins:
"And first to you, my dear wife, I do with all the strength
and powers that is in me, thank you for your kindness

and faithfulness to me." No doubt Asael stated their joint ideal in his advice on parenthood for his own children: "Make it your chiefest work to bring them up in the ways of virtue that they may be useful in their generation."[190] From a family of courageous Revolutionary soldiers, Mary Duty distinguished herself in rearing eleven children.[191] She was an example of industry to her family, for John remembered his mother as "a first-rate dairy woman."[192]

No doubt Mary was also a first-rate mother. Her physical record is impressive enough, for children came annually in the first two years after marriage, then every other year until the move from New Hampshire to Massachusetts in 1786; four years later the eleventh and last arrived.[193] Her family had superior care or health for its time, since all children lived to maturity. Certain other patterns appear in this group. Educational exposure was marginal in New Hampshire and Vermont, but native intelligence is plain. Eldest Jesse took his father's place in Tunbridge as a civic leader, holding most offices, including selectman and town clerk.[194] Next son Joseph Smith, Sr., was less outgoing, but he taught school as well as farmed in his New England years.[195] Asael, Jr., Silas, and John became Mormons and were known as able people. Asael, Jr., had been a Vermont militia lieutenant, and after conversion served on two high councils before ordination as patriarch—he died in Iowa during the Mormon exodus.[196] Silas had been a Vermont militia captain, and after conversion became a high priest before his untimely death in Illinois.[197] Younger brother John made his mark as a church leader—in the First Presidency in Ohio, in local and regional presidencies in Missouri and Illinois, and in Utah as the first Salt Lake stake president. He was also an articulate patriarch, whose letters and journals (including the extract reproduced in chapter 7) show good literacy and intellectual capacity.[198] The "will" of Asael Smith, Sr., proves that the parents valued excellence, even though substantial education was denied their children until the maturity of youngest brother Stephen. Then death intervened. Asael and Mary's own ambitions, in some measure transmitted to each child, are clearly stated in Stephen's unusual obituary of 1802:

> Died, at Royalton, on the 25th ult., Mr. Stephen Smith, aged 17, the seventh son of Mr. Asael Smith, of Tunbridge; he was designed for a public education and had made some proficiency in his study. By this stroke of providence, his parents are deprived of a very promising son, cut down in the bloom of his youth like the tender grass, in whom they anticipated great comfort. He has left 6 brothers and 4 sisters to mourn the loss of a pleasing brother, whose amiable disposition had united their most tender affections towards him. He was the ornament of his parents, the pride of his brethren, and the admiration of all his acquaintance. But alas, he is no more! The virtuous are not exempt from the destroyer.[199]

Had he lived, Stephen probably would have enrolled in the Royalton Academy, which six months before his death had sought to locate on the "meeting house green."[200] A happier event came earlier that year—the marriage of Asael, Jr., to a Royalton girl. In fact, Stephen's loss in 1802 was tempered by satisfaction in about a dozen grandchildren. Eldest son Jesse had married a Tunbridge girl in 1792, followed by Joseph, Sr., in 1796. That was the year of three marriages, when eldest daughters Priscilla and Mary wedded men of prominent Royalton families. Later years brought additional marriages of Asael and Mary's children, including the joining of John Smith and Clarissa Lyman, from a notable New England family.[201] In his Family Address Asael had reason to state that "nature will find its own."

Where evidence exists, the children of Asael and Mary were generally church members, and the men of the family could handle the Bible as skillfully as an axe. George A. recalled early family discussion about the Book of Mormon and evaluated the scriptural knowledge of Asael Smith, Jr.:

[He] was a man of extraordinary retentive memory, and pos-sessed a great knowledge of the Bible, so much so that he could read it as well without the book as with it. And after he embraced "Mormonism," nobody could oppose him successfully, for all their objections were answered from the Bible immediately, giving chap-ter and verse.[202]

Such careful study was a family pattern. George A. Smith also remembered the first preaching of his father, John, after conversion to Mormonism: "Our neighbors were astonished at his knowledge of the Bible."[203]

The Smiths were religiously committed but open-minded. The notable exception was Jesse, entrenched in Calvinistic theology; in 1836 two brothers were ordered not to talk "about the Bible at all in his house unless it was upon limited election."[204] However, the family tended more toward the position of second son, Joseph Smith, Sr.—devoted to scripture but consciously seeking something more satisfying than formal creeds. His intense search for God set him apart from his brothers and sis-ters, for he was too religious to commit himself to any church.[205] Asael, Mary, and eight of their children were still alive when the Book of Mormon was first brought to their areas. Only Jesse and two sisters failed to be-lieve.[206]

Life's sunset for Asael and Mary Duty Smith was west of Vermont.[207] Census takers found them in Tunbridge, Vermont, in 1800 and 1810, but they appear in Stock-holm, St. Lawrence County, New York, on the 1820 and 1830 censuses.[208] Their son Joseph Smith, Sr., and his family had moved to western New York about 1816, but at this period Asael and his other sons ventured to new lands in northern New York.[209] There the aged parents and families of six children gradually gathered, again successful on their farms and in maintaining family unity.[210] But severe conflict came when Joseph Smith, Sr., wrote in the fall of 1828, sharing "several remark-able visions" of Joseph Smith, Jr. Though pressing ninety, Asael firmly withstood the opposition of his sons, who at first "ridiculed Joseph's visions": "The old gentleman said that he always knew that God was going to raise up some branch of his family to be a great benefit to mankind."[211] George A. Smith remembered such words. He was then a studious teenager who paid strict attention to his grandfather, and later recalled Asael's belief "that something would turn up in his family that would revolutionize the world."[212] Asael had long held that kind of conviction, for his 1796 letter had portrayed God's program to obliterate all "ecclesiastical tyranny."

Eldest Jesse fiercely sought to shield his father from news of the revelations of Joseph Smith, Jr. However, he bitterly conceded the ineffectiveness of his ridicule, complaining in a letter to Hyrum Smith: "your good, pious, and Methodistical Uncle Asael induced his father to give credit to your tale of nonsense."[213] Asael, Sr., died in 1830, but not until his son Joseph Smith, Sr., had visited him personally with the newly published Book of Mormon. Like the elder brother of the prodigal son, Jesse was enraged. In fact, he openly threatened the Prophet's father if he continued to mention "such blasphemous stuff." Other brothers were cordial, though cautious. However, John's early account pictures aged Asael warmly responding to the message of his second son:

> After the usual salutations, inquiries, and explanations, the subject of the Book of Mormon was introduced. Father received with gladness that which Joseph [Sr.] communicated and remarked that he had always expected that something would appear to make known the true gospel.[214]

Asael Smith's sons took time to weigh carefully this new message. Their father led out in accepting it, though he "had been for many years a Universalist and exceedingly set in his way."[215] Grandson George A. Smith left a glimpse of Asael's final months: "My grandfather Asael fully believed the Book of Mormon, which he read nearly through, although in his eighty-eighth year, without the aid of glasses."[216] He died that fall, confident that a new religious age was upon the world.[217]

In his "will" Asael Smith spoke comfort to his widow, and his intuition of preceding her in death proved correct. She lived to see three of four surviving sons accept the new faith, beginning with the dramatic baptism of John Smith in an iced-over stream in early January 1832. John returned to northern New York as a missionary in 1833 and visited surviving Mary Duty Smith: "Went to see my old mother, who is in the ninetieth year of her age. Found her in health, much pleased to see us."[218]

Vitality, affection, and spirituality are the closing impressions of her life. Her son Silas remained in St. Lawrence County until 1836, and her grandson Hyrum wrote to insist:

It is the will of God that Uncle Silas should fetch grandmother in spite of all the devils there are out of hades. And God will bless him in so doing and give her strength to endure the journey. And we will help him take care of her whenever he arrives here.[219]

The nearly ninety-three-year-old matriarch willingly endured a 500-mile journey, for "she had asked the Lord that she might live to see her children and grandchildren once more."[220] She migrated to Kirtland in May 1836 with the northern New York saints, families of Asael Smith, Jr., Silas Smith, and other converts. Elias Smith, son of Asael, Jr., particularly cared for his grandmother in the second half of her journey. His contemporary journal gives geographical details of the week-long voyage down the St. Lawrence River and Lake Ontario to Rochester, where Mary Duty Smith went on by Erie Canal boat to Buffalo, transferring to the steamboat *Sandusky* for the final cruise across Lake Erie to Fairport, a dozen miles from her destination of Kirtland. They landed "about 5 p.m.," and soon fair skies turned to rain. Although

Elias' journal outlines these events, he later gave details
of Mary Smith's reunion with her grandsons Joseph and
Hyrum:

> During the landing of the company, he sat her on the wharf to
> give her fresh air. But a shower coming on, he sought a public
> house nearby for a room for her during the night, but was refused;
> whereupon he went to a hotel on the same block and was cordially
> treated. While he was taking his grandmother to the hotel, Joseph
> the Prophet, his brother Hyrum, and [F.] G. Williams from Kirtland
> came down to the wharf to meet them. They followed to the hotel,
> and Joseph and Hyrum went into the room to see their grandmother,
> but would not make themselves known that night. They left their
> grandmother there for the night in comfortable quarters, and with
> their cousin Elias returned to Kirtland in the midst of the storm,
> arriving very late. Next morning they took carriage and drove down
> for their grandmother, while Elias hired teams and went down to
> the emigrants, whom he had sheltered for the night in a warehouse.
> The meeting between the grandmother and her prophet-descendant
> and his brother was most touching. Joseph blessed her and said
> she was the most honored woman on earth. She had desired to see
> all her children and grandchildren before she died, which with
> one exception was providentially granted her.[221]

Attention focused on Mary Duty Smith in the family
reunions at Kirtland, and she glowed with enthusiasm.
Writing at the time, conservative Elias Smith captured
the happiness of that May 17:

> [W]ent to Fairport with Joseph and Hyrum after grandmother.
> Found her well and as smart as I have ever seen her for ten years.
> The day was fine after the rain of the preceding evening, and
> everything seemed to welcome her to this country. Joseph brought
> her in his carriage from Fairport, and Hyrum and some other
> brethren from Kirtland moved the brethren to Kirtland, where they
> all arrived safe toward evening. Grandmother was overjoyed at
> meeting her children, grandchildren, etc., in this place, whom she
> had not seen for many years, and many of them she had never had
> the satisfaction of beholding.[222]

Lucy Smith remembered her mother-in-law's "good
health and excellent spirits" on arrival, when "she re-

joiced to meet so many of her children, grandchildren, and great grandchildren."[223] Beyond kinship, there was the religious meaning of her pilgrimage, for Mary Duty Smith completely accepted the testimony of her grandson-prophet. She told Lucy Smith, "I am going to have your Joseph [Jr.] baptize me, and my Joseph [the patriarch] bless me."[224]

Young Eliza R. Snow watched Asael Smith's widow closely and felt that she looked twenty years younger, "in appearance not over seventy-five." Eliza was near Mary Smith in her last few days in Ohio and penned the final pictures of the Prophet's grandmother. After years apart, the Smith family gathered, and Mary was the life of the party:

> The next day after her arrival at the house of the Prophet, where she was welcomed with every manifestation of kindness and affection, her children, grandchildren and great-grandchildren— all who were residents of Kirtland, and two of her sons, who arrived with her—came together to enjoy with her a social family meeting. And a happy one it was—a season of pure reciprocal conviviality, in which her buoyancy of spirit greatly augmented the general joy. Let the reader imagine for a moment this aged matron, surrounded by her four sons, Joseph, Asael, Silas and John, all of them, as well as several of her grandsons, upwards of six feet in height, with a score of great-grandchildren of various sizes intermixed.[225]

"I wish she had set the time longer" was Joseph Smith's earlier reaction to news of his grandmother's arrival, a premonition fulfilled within two weeks.[226] About sunset on May 27, 1836, she died, and Eliza R. Snow "was with her, and saw her calmly fall asleep." About ten minutes before death, Mary Duty Smith identified a group of supernatural beings visible to her: "pointing towards them she exclaimed, 'O, how beautiful! But they do not speak!' "[227] Thus both grandmothers of the Prophet passed from mortality with firm convictions of the world to come. They had walked with God in life and trusted him in death. One cannot doubt that their homes had contained the virtues that Solomon Mack thanked his wife for instilling into his children: "piety, gentleness, and reflection."

CHAPTER 6

Writings of Asael Smith

Both of the major known writings of Asael Smith are printed in full here in chronological order. The personal letter of 1796 reveals Asael as a God-fearing, hard-working entrepreneur, with a warm relationship with his family and friends plus a streak of purposeful humor. The Family Address of 1799 shows the depth of his idealism, Christian conviction, and practical religion. Both the man in society and his personal values are seen in the two holographs, which capture him as a mature man in his fifties. In addition to these documents, the biographical chapter and notes print in full all known minor writings, with the exception of his genealogical annotations. Facsimiles of the original documents are reproduced after the transcription of each, the letter by courtesy of Essex Institute, Salem, Massachusetts—and the Family Address by courtesy of the LDS Church Historian Howard W. Hunter. In printing these two sources, misspellings have been corrected, though period spellings are largely retained. Punctuation and capitalization have been altered for clarity, though such changes are imposed conservatively. Brackets indicate either editorial additions or editorial reconstruction of a reading where the paper is broken off or aged. In making such judgments, President Joseph Fielding Smith's printing in 1902 (listed in the bibliography) has been persuasive, since he read and transcribed the address almost seventy years before its present condition. For identification of the personalities of the letter, see the biographical chapter on Asael Smith, including notes 158 to 163. Personal names follow spelling in the letter, though variants occur regularly in this period; Jacob Towne's name follows the spelling preferred in family documents.

ASAEL SMITH'S LETTER TO JACOB TOWNE

Tunbridge, Jan. 14th, 1796

Respected Sir:

Having a favorable opportunity, altho on very short notice, I with joy and gratitude embrace it, returning herewith my most hearty thanks for your respect shown in your favor of the 30th of November by Mr. Wildes, which I view as a singular specimen of friendship which has very little been practiced by any of my friends in Topsfield, altho often requested.

My family is all, through the goodness of the divine benediction, in a tolerable good state of health, and desire to be remembered to you and to all inquiring friends.

I have set me up a new house since Mr. Wildes was here, and expect to remove into it next spring and to begin again on an entire new farm. And my son Joseph will live on the old farm (if this that has been but four years occupied can be called old) and carry it on at the halves, which half I hope will nearly furnish my family with food, whilst I with my four youngest sons shall endeavor to bring to another farm, etc.

As to news, I have nothing, as I know of, worth noticing, except that grain has taken a sudden rise amongst us, about one-third.

As to the Jacobin party, they are not very numerous here, or if they are, they are pretty still. There is some in this state, viz., in Bennington, who, like other children crying for a rattle, have blared out against their rulers in hopes to wrest from them if possible what they esteem, the plaything of power and trust. But they have been pretty well whip't and have become tolerably quiet again. And I am in hopes, if they live to arrive to the years of discretion, when the empire of reason shall take place, that they will then become good members of society, notwithstanding their noisy, nauseous behavior in their childhood, for which they was neither capable of hearing or giving any reason.

For my part, I am so willing to trust the government of the world in the hands of the Supreme Ruler of universal nature, that I do not at present wish to try to wrest it out of his hands. And I have so much confidence in his abilities to teach our senators wisdom that I do not think it worthwhile for me to interpose, from the little stock of knowledge that he has favored me with, in the affair, either one way or the other. He has conducted us through a glorious revolution and has brought us into the promised land of peace and liberty. And I believe that he is about to bring all the world into the same beatitude in his own time and way, which, altho his ways may appear [ever] so inconsistent to our blind reason, yet may be perfectly consistent with his designs. And I believe that the stone is now cut out of the mountain without hands, spoken of by Daniel, and has smitten the image upon his feet, by which the iron, the clay, the brass, the silver and the gold—viz., all monarchial and ecclesiastical tyranny—will be broken to pieces an[d] become as the chaff of the summer thrashing floor. The wind shall carry them all away that there shall be no place found for them.

Give my best regards to your parents, and tell them that I have taken up with the eleventh commandment, that the Negro taught to the minister, which was thus:

The minister asked the Negro how many commandments there was; his answer was, "Eleben, sir." "Aye," replied the other: "What is the eleventh? That is one I never heard of." "The elebenth commandment, sir, is mind your own business."

So I choose to do, and give myself but little concerns about what passes in the political world.

Give my best regards to Dr. Meriam, Mr. Wildes, Joseph Dorman, and Mr. Cree, and tell Mr. Cree I thank him for his respects and hope he will accept of mine. Write to me as often and as large as you can and oblige your sincere friend and well wisher,

Asael Smith

Mr. Jacob Towne, Jr.

[Back of the first page of the letter:]

Give my hearty thanks to Mr. Charles Rogers for his respect shown in writing me a few lines, and tell him that I should a wrote to him now, had I had time, but now waive it for the present, as I have considerable part of what I intend to a writ to you.

If I should live and do well, I expect to come to Topsfield myself next winter, which, if I do, I shall come and pay you a visit. Farewell.

Tell Mr. Joseph Cree that if he will come here and set up his trade, I will warrant him as much work as he can do, and good pay.

[Margin of the second page of the letter:]

I expect my son Joseph will be married in a few days.

Sunbridge Jan^r 14th 1796

Respected Sir

Having a favorable opertunity altho on very
short notice, I with joy & gratitude imbrace it;
Returning herewith my most harty thanks for your
respect I have in your favor of the 30th of Novr by
mr Gilly which I view as a singular specimen of
friendship which has very Little been practised by aney
of my frinds in Topsfield, altho often requested

My family is all, threw the goodness of the
Divine benidiction, in a Tolarable good state of health and
desier to be remembred to you and to all inquiring frinds

I have set me up a new house, since mr Willa
was hear, and Expect to remove into it, next spring, and
to begin again on an intire new farme, and my son Joseph
will live on the old ———— farme, (if this that has been but 4
years can be called old) and carry it on at the halves which
half I hope will nearly furnish my famely with food, whilst
I with my four youngest sons shall indeavur to bring to
a neither farme &c

as to news, I have nothing as I know of, worth
noticing, except that grain has taken a sudden rise amongst
us about one third

as to the Jacobine perty they are not very numerous hear, or if they are they are pretty still, there
is some in this state (viz) in Bennington, who Like other
children crying for a Rattle have blared out against there
Rulers, in hopes to rest from them if posable, what they
Esteem, the plaything of power, & trust, but they have
been pretty well whipt, and have become Tolarabley
Quiet again and I am in hopes if they live to arrive to the
years of disgresion when the Empier of reason, shall take
place, that they will then becom good members of Society,
notwithstanding their noisey nuicious behaviour in their
child hood, for which they was neither capable of hearing,
or giving aney reason

for my part I am so willing to trust the government
of the world in the hands of the supream ruler of uni
versal nature, that I do not at present wish to tryte
wrest it out of his hands, and I have so much Confidence
in his abilities to teach our Senators wisdom that I
do not think it worth while for me to interpose from
the little stock of knowledge that he has favord me
with in the affair either one way or the
other, he has conducted us thro' a glorious revolution
and has brought us into the promised Land of peace
& Liberty, and I believe that he is about to bring all
the world into the same Beatitude in his own time & way
which, altho his ways may appear, never so inconsistant
to our blind reasons yet may be perfectly consistent with
his Designs. and I believe that the Stone is now cut out
of the mountain without hands spoken of by Daniel and has
smitten the image upon his feet By which the iron, the
Clay, the Brass, the Silver, & the Gold (vis) all monarical,
and Eclesiastical Tirony) will be Broken to peaces as
Becom as the Chaff of the Summer Thrashing Flore,
the wind shall carry them all away that there shall
be no place found for them
            give my best regards to your parents and tell
them that I have taken up with the Eleventh Commandment
that the Negro taught to the minister,   which thus
            the minister asked the Negro how many
Comandments there wos, his answare wos, Eleven Sir,
aye reployd the other, what is the Eleventh, that
is one I never heard of ———— the Eleventh Com
mandment, Sir, is, mind your own Buisness,
            So I chuse to do, and give my self but Little
Concerne about what passes in the political world
            give my Best regards to Dr merian, mr willes,
Joseph Dorman, and mr Cree and tell mr Cree I thank him
for his respects and hope he will ———— accept of mine,
write to me as often & as Large as you can and oblige y[or]
Sincear friend & well wisher   Asael Smith
mr Jacob Town Jur

POSTSCRIPTS OF THE JACOB TOWNE, JR.,
LETTER, THE SECOND WRITTEN VERTICALLY
IN THE MARGIN OF THE SIGNATURE PAGE

ASAEL SMITH'S ADDRESS TO HIS FAMILY

A few words of advice, which I leave to you, my dear wife and children, whom I expect ere long to leave:

My Dear Selfs,

I know not what leisure I shall have at the hour of my death to speak unto you, and as you all know that I am not free in speech, especially when sick or sad; and therefore now [d]o speak my heart to you, and would wish you to hear me speaking to you as long as you live (when my tongue shall be mouldered to dust in the silent tomb) in this my writing, which I divide among you all.

And first to you, my dear wife, I do with all the strength and powers that is in me, thank you for your kindness and faithfulness to me, beseeching God, who is the husband of the widow, to take care of you and not to leave you nor forsake you, nor never suffer you to leave nor forsake him nor his [way]s. Put your whole trust solely [in him. He neve]r did nor never will forsake any that trusted in him. One thing, however, I would add, if you should marry again. Remember what I have undergone by a stepmother, and do not estrange your husband from his own children or kindred, lest you draw on him and on yourself a great sin. So I do resign you into the everlasting arms of the great husband of husbands, the Lord Jesus Christ.

And now my dear children, let me pour out my heart to you and speak first to you of immortality in your souls. Trifle not in this point: the soul is immortal. You have to deal with an infinite majesty; you go upon life and death. Therefore, in this point be serious. Do all to God in a serious manner. When you think of him, speak of him, pray to him, or in any way make your addresses to his great majesty, be in good earnest. Trifle not with his name

nor with his attributes, nor call him to witness to anything but is absolute truth; nor then, but when sound
reason on serious consideration requires it. And as to
religion, I would not wish to point out any particular
form to you; but first I would wish you to search
the scriptures and consult sound [reas]on, and see if they
(which I take to [be] two witnesses that stand by the
God of the whole earth) are not sufficient to evince to
you that religion is a necessary theme. Then I would wish
you to study the nature of religion, and see whether it
consists in outward formalities, or in the hidden man of
the heart; whether you can by outward forms, rites and
ordinances save yourselves, or whether there is a necessity
of your having help from any other hand than your own.
If you find that you stand in need of a Savior, Christ
saith: "Look unto me and be ye saved all ye ends of the
earth." Then look to him, and if you find from scripture
and sound reason that Christ hath come into the world to
save sinners, then examine what it was that caused him
to leave the center of consummate happiness to suffer as
he did—whether it was to save mankind because they were
sinners and could not save themselves or whether he [came]
to save mankind because they had repented of their
sins, so as to be forgiven on the score of their repentance. If you find that he came to save sinners merely
because they were such, then try if there is any other
so great that he cannot save him. But mind that you
admit no others as evidences but the two that God hath
appointed, viz., scripture and sound reason. And if these
two witness that you are one whit better by nature than
the worst heathen in the darkest corner of the deserts
of Arabia, then conclude that God hath been partial towards you and hath furnished you with a better nature
than others; and that consequently, he is not just to all
mankind. But if these two witnesses testify to you that
God is just to all, and his tender mercies are over all
his works; then believe them. And if you can believe that

Christ [came] to save sinners and not the righteous Phari-
sees or self-righteous; that sinners must be saved by the
righteousness of Christ alone, without mixing any of
their own righteousness with his, then you will see that
he can as well save all as any. And there is no respect of
persons with God, who will have all mankind to be
saved and come to the knowledge of the truth, viz., that
"there is one God and one mediator between God and
man, the man Christ Jesus, who gave himself a ransom
for all, to be testified in due time." And when you believe this you will enter into his rest, and when you
enter into his rest you will know what that rest is, and
not before. And having gotten this evidence that God is
true, be still adding to your evidence and enjoy your
present assurance. Do all to God as to your father, for
his love is ten thousand times greater towards you than
ever any earthly father's could [be] to his offspring.

In the next place strive for these graces most which
concern your places and conditions, and strive most
against those failings which most threaten you. But above
everything avoid a melancholy disposition. That is a
humor that admits of any temptation and is capable of
any impression and distemper. Shun as death this humor,
which will work you to all unthankfulness against God,
unlovingness to men, and unnaturalness to yourselves
and one another.

Do not talk and make a noise to get the name of forward men, but do the thing and do it in a way that is
fair and honest, which you can live and die by and rise
and reign by. Therefore, my children, do more than you
talk of, in point of religion. Satisfy your own consciences
in what you do. All men you shall never satisfy; nay,
some will not be satisfied though they be convinced.

As for Your Callings: Any honest calling will honor
you if you honor that. It is better to be a rich cobbler
than a poor merchant; a rich farmer than a poor preacher.

And never be discouraged, though sometimes your schemes should not succeed according to your wishes.

Persevere in the way of well-doing, and you may hope for success. For myself, I (who had never your parts nor helps)—I never found anything too hard for me in my calling but discouragement and unbelief. If I was discouraged and did not believe I could do a thing, I never could. Therefore, when you think anything is too hard for you, do not undertake it.

As to Your Company: Abandon all infectious, flattering, self-serving companions. When once you have found them false, trust them no more. Sort with such as are able to do or receive good. Solomon gives you the best counsel for this in many places. Read the Proverbs and remember him in this. Forsake not an old friend; be friendly and faithful to your friends. Never trouble nor trust friends unless there be a necessity; and lastly, be long in closing with friends and loath to loose them upon experience of them.

As to Your Marriages: I do not think it worthwhile to say much about them, for I believe God hath created the persons for each other, and that nature will find its own.

But for Your Children: Make it your chiefest work to bring them up in the ways of virtue that they may be useful in their generation. Give them if possible a good education. If nature hath made no difference, do you make none in your affections, countenances nor portions; partiality this way begets envy, hatred, strife and contention.

And as for Yourselves Within Yourselves: My desire hath been to carry an even hand towards you all, and I have labored to reduce you as near as I could (all circumstances considered) to an equality. And therefore, my last request and charge is that you will live together in an undivided bond of love. You are many of you, and if you join together as one man, you need not want anything. What counsel, what comfort, what money, what friends may you not help yourselves unto, if you will all as one contribute your aids.

Wherefore my dear children, I pray, beseech, and adjure you by all the relations and dearness that hath ever been betwixt us and by the heart-rending pangs of a dying father, whose soul hath been ever bound in the bundle of life with yours, that you know one another. Visit as you may each other. Comfort, counsel, relieve, succor, help and admonish one another. And while your mother lives, meet her if possible once every year. When she is dead, pitch on some other place, if it may be, your elder brother's house; or if you cannot meet, send to and hear from each other yearly and oftener if you can. And when you have neither father nor mother left, be so many fathers and mothers to each other, so you shall understand the blessing mentioned in the 133 Psalm.

As to Your Estates: Be not troubled that you are below your kindred. Get more wisdom, humility and virtue, and you are above them—only do this. Deal with your hearts to make them less. Begin low, join together to help one another. Rest upon the promises which are many and precious this way. Love mercy, and have mercy on yourselves and on on[e] another, and I know— I know, I say, and I am confident in it, that if you will trust God in his own way, he will make comfortable provisions for you. Make no more objections, but trust him.

For the Public: Bless God that you live in a land of liberty, and bear yourselves dutifully and conscionably towards the authority under which you live. See God's providence in the appointment of the Federal Constitution, and hold union and order as a precious jewel. And for the Church of Christ: neither set her above her husband nor below her children; give her that honor, obedience and respect that is her due. And if you will be my children and heirs of my comfort in my dying age, be neither another's nor factious of any party or faction or novelty. It is true, this is not a rising way, but it is a free, fair, comfortable way for a man to follow his own judgment without wavering to either hand.

I make no doubt but you will hear divers opinions concerning me, both before and after I shall sleep in silence; but do not be troubled at that. I did what in my circumstances seemed best for me for the present; however, the event hath not in some points answered my expectation. Yet I have learned to measure things by another rule than events and satisfy myself in this, that I did all for the best as I thought. And if I had not so much foresight as some others, I cannot help it.

Sure I am my Savior, Christ, is perfect, and never will fail in one circumstance. To him I commit your souls, bodies, estates, names, characters, lives, deaths and all—and myself, waiting when he shall change my vile body and make it like his own most glorious body. And [I] wish to leave to you everything that I have in this world but my faults, and them I take with me to the grave, there to be buried in everlasting oblivion; but leaving my virtues, if ever I had any, to revive and live in you. Amen. So come, Lord Jesus; come quickly. Amen.

The above was written April the 10th, 1799 and left for my dearly beloved wife and children to view after my decease.

Asael Smith

A few words of advice
which I Leave to you my
Dear wife and Children whome
I Expect ear Long to Leave

MY Dear Selfs,
I know not what Leisure I shall
have at the hower of my Death to
Speak unto you, and as you all know
that I am not free in Speach especially when Sick, or Sad: and therefore now to Speak my heart to you
and would wish you to hear me
Speaking to you as Long as you
Live, (when my Tongue shall be
mouldered to Dust in the Silant troun
in this my writing which I Leave
among you all.

and first to you my Dear
wife, I Do with all the Strength an
powers that is in me, thank you
for your kindness and faithfullness
to me, Beseeching God, who is the
[ ]band of the wi[ ]s to take Care
of you and not to Leave you nor
for Sake you, nor never suffer you
[ ] Leave nor forsake him [ ]
[ ] put your whole tru[ ]
[ ] Ded nor never will [ ]

aney, that trusted in him, one thing
however I would add, if you Should Marry
again, remember what I have undergon
by a Step mother, and Do not litrage(?)
your husband from his own children
or kindred, Leest you Draw on him
and on your Silf a great Sin —
So I Do resign you into the Everlasting armes of the great husband
of husbands the Lord Jesus Christ.

and Now my Dear Children Let me
pour out my heart to you and speak dire
to you of immortality in your Souls.

trifel not in this point, the Soul is
immortal, you have to Deal with an infi-
nit Majesty, you go upon Life and Death,
therefore in this point be Serious; Do all
to god in a Serious mannor. when you
think of him, Speak of him, pray to him
or in aney way make your addresses to
his great majesty, Be in good Earnist.
trifel not with his name nor with his
attributs, nor Call him to witness to aney
thing, but is absolute truth, nor then, but
when Sound reason, on Serious Consideratio
requiers it. and as to religion I would
not wish to point out aney perticuler forme
to you, but first I would wish you to
the Scriptures, and Consult Sound
and See if they (which I take to
two witnesses that Stand by

the god of the whole Earth) are not
Sufficeant to Evince to you, that religion is a Neecsessary theam, then
I would wish you to Studdy the Nature
of religion, and See whether it consisits
in outward formalities, or in the hidden
man of the heart, whether you can by
outward formes, rites, and ordenances. Save
your Selves, or whether there is a Necessity
of your having help from any other hand
than your own, if you fiend that you Stand in Need of a Saviour, christ Saith Look
unto me and be ye Saved all ye endes of the
Eartha then Loot to him, and if you
fiend from Scripture and Sound reason
that Christ hath come into the world to
Save Sinners, then Examin in what it was
that caused him to Leave the center of
consumate happyness, to Suffer as he did
whether it was to Save mankind because they ware Sinners and could not
Save themselves, or whether he come
to Save mankind because they had
repented of their Sins Soas to be forgiven on the Scoar of their repentance.
if you fiend that he came to Save
Sinners, mearly because they
su... then try if there is

so great that he cannot save him.
but oriend that ~~thes~~ you admit no
others as Evidences, but the two that
god thath apointed (viz) Scripture &
sound reason. and if these two witness
that you are one whit better by nature
than the worst heathen in the Darkest corner of the Desarts of arabia,
then conclude that god hath been partial toards you, and hath furnished
you with a better Nature than others
and that (consequently he is not Just
to all man-kind. but if these two
witneses, testify to you that god is Just
to all, and his tender marcies are over
all his workes, then believe them.
and if you can believe that Christ
come to save sinners and not the
rightious, pharesees, or ~~y~~ self rightei-
ous. ~~or one~~ that sinners must be
saved by the rightiousness of Christ
aktne, without mixing aney of
their own rightiousness with his;
    then you will see that he can
as well save all, as aney, and there
is no respect of persons with god, who
~~wil~~ have all mankind to be saved and
~~to~~ the knowledg of the truth

(viz) that there is one god, and
one mediator between god and man
the Man Christ Jesus who gave himself a ransome for all, to be testifyed
in Dee time. and when you Believe
this you will Enter into his rest.
and when you Enter into his rest
you will know what that rest is,
and not before. and having got
the this Evidence that god is true be
still adding to your Evidence and
injoy your present assurance; do
all to god as to your father, for
his Love is ten thousand times grea-
tor toards you, than ever any
earthly fathers could to his offspring.

in the Next place strive for
those graces most, which concern
your places and conditions, and
strive most against those failings which most threaten you;
But above every thing avoid a Mela-
ancolly Disposition, that is a hum-
er that admits of every temptation and is capable of any

impression and Distemper, shun as
Death this humour, which will work
you to all unthankfulness against god,
unlovingness to men, and unnaturalness to your Selves, and one another.

Do not talk and make a noise
to git the name of forward Men,
But Do the things; and Do it in a
way that is fair and honest which
you can Live and Die by; and rise
and raygn by; therefore my Children
Do more than you talk of in point
of religion; Satisfy your own consciences in what you Do; all Men
you shall never Satisfie, nay, some
will not be Satisfied though they be
convinced.

as for your callings
aney honest calling will honour
you, if you honour that; it is better
to be a rich Cobler than a poor Marchant,
a rich fermor than a poor preacher,
and Never be Discouraged, though
sometimes your Scheames should not
suceed according to your wishes,
passivear in the way of welldoing and
you may hope for success, for my
self I who had never your parts nor

helpless. Never found any thing too hard for me in my Calling, but Discouragement and unbileaf. if I was Discouraged and Did not believe I could Do a thing, I never could. therefore when you think any thing is too hard for you, Do not undertake it.

as to your Company abandon all infectious, flattering, self-serving companions; when once you have found them false, trust them no more. Sort with such as are able to Do or receive good. Solomon gives you the best counsel for this in many places. read the Provarbs, and remumber him in this forsake not an old friend, be friendly, and faithful to your friends. Never trouble nor trust friends unless there be a Necessity. and Lastly, be Long in closing with friends, and Loth to Loose them upon experience of them.

as to your marriages I Do not think it worth while to Say much about them for I believe God hath created the parsons for each other; and that Nature will find its own. But for your Children.

make it your cheapest work to bring them up in the ways of Virtue

that they may be usefull in their generation. give them if posable a good education,
if nature hath made no differance, do
you make none in your affections, countenances, nor portions; partiallity, this way
Begets envy, hatred, strife and contention
and as for your Selves within your Selves.

my desier hath been to carry an even
hand toards you all, and I have Labour-
ed to reduce you, as Near as I could (all
circumstances considered) to an equall-
ity, and therefore my Last request &
charge is, that you will Live together
in an undivided bond of Love; you
are maney of you, and if you Join together as one man, you need not want any
thing; what counsil, what comfort, what
money, what friends may you not help
your Selves unto, if you will, all as one contribute your aids? wherefore my dear
Children, I pray, Beseech, and adjure
you, by all the relations and dearness
that hath Ever been betwixt us, and
by the heart rending pangs of a
Dying father, whos Soul hath been
ever bound in the bundle of Life with
yours. that you know one anoth-
visit (as you may) each other

Comfort, counsel, relieve, Succour, help and admonish one another. and while your mother Lives, meet hear (if posably) once Every year. when She is Dead, pitch on Some other place; if it may be, your Elder Brothers house; or if you Cannot meet, Send tor and hear from each other yearly, and oftener if you Can. and when you have Nuther father nor mother Left, be so many vathers and mothers to each other, So you shall understand the blessing mentioned in the 133 psalm

as to your Estates

Be not troubled that you are below your kindred; git more wisdom, humility, and virtue, and you are above them; only Do this, 1 Deal with your hearts to make them Less, Begin Low, Join together to help one another, rest upon the promises, which are many, and precious this way. Love marcy, and have marcy on your Selves, and on on another, and I know I know, I say, and I am Confident, in it, that if you will trust god in his own ways, he will make Comfortable provisions for you. Make no more objections, But trust him.

for the publie.

Bless god that you Live in a Land of Liberty, and bex bear your Selves Dutifully, and conjonably toards the authority under whe

you Live, See gods providence in the appoi
nent of the Federal Constitution, and hold
vnion and order as a precious Iewel!
and for the Church of Christ, Neither
Set her above her husband, nor below her
Children; give her that honour, obedience,
and respect that is her Due; and if you
will be my Children, and heirs of my Comfo
rt in my Dying age, be neither a nothers,
nor factious of any party or faction or novilty.
it is true, this is not a resing way; but it is
a Free, fair, comfortable way for a man
to follow his own Iudgement without warp
ing to Either hand. I make no Doubt
but you will hear Divers opinions conser
ning Me, Both before, and after I shall
Sleep in Silence, but Do not be troubled
at that, I did what, in my circumstances
Seemed best for me for the present;
how ever the event hath not in some pointe
answered My Expectation, yet I have
Larned to measure things by a nother rule
then events, and Satisfy my self in this
that I did all for the best, as I thought,
and if I had not so much fore-sight as
Some others, I cannot help it.
        Sure I am my Saviour Christ is par-
fect and Never will fail in one circomstance
To him I commit your Souls, bodies,
estates, names, carractere, Living, Dea'ths

and, all; and my Self wating when
he Shall change my vile body and
make its Like his own most glorious
Body. and wish to Leave to you every
thing that I have in this World but my
folts, and them I take with me to
the grave, there to be buried in everlasting oblivion. but Leaving my vertues
of ever I had aneys to rivive and live
in ajou. Amen So Come Lord Jesus
Come Quickly Amen

        the Above was written April
the 10th 1799 and Left for my
Dearly Beloved wife and Children
to view after my Deseas

                    Asael Smith

CHAPTER 7

John Smith's Family History

Asael Smith thought it remarkable that teenage grandson George A. Smith would sit and question him about early family events. This historical interest continued in George A. Smith to later years, when his discourses were incident-centered as counselor to Brigham Young and much of his time was given to his position as Church Historian. Earlier the Mormon people had been ordered from their Missouri homes during fateful 1838. After that crisis, George A. Smith pressed his father to record the family story, against the risk that he might die and his knowledge perish with him. John Smith began this record from childhood memories and no doubt included events that his father, Asael, had intimately related to him (cp. n. 240). The result is the only narrative of Asael Smith's life and of the early years of his children. Ending in his middle age, it features Asael's sacrifice to uphold family honor by meeting his father's obligations. John Smith's emphasis on that episode shows how Asael Smith's honesty impressed his sons.

The author of this history was a man of independence and ability. Principle, not conformity, governed his life, as illustrated by two incidents. "I want to thank you; your father saved my life," an elderly lady told George A. Smith upon his visit to Potsdam, New York, in 1872: "we were broken through the ice into the lake, and at the risk of his own life he saved mine."[228] John Smith would risk both physical safety and social acceptance. When his oldest brother, Jesse, warned that his brothers were "setting a trap" to make him believe

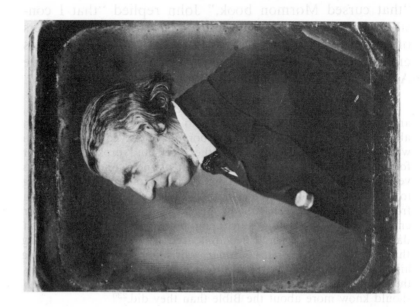

JOHN SMITH
SON OF ASAEL SMITH

GEORGE A. SMITH
SON OF JOHN SMITH

"that cursed Mormon book," John replied "that I considered myself amply able to judge for myself in matters of religion."[229] Just the story òf his January baptism is enough to shock the faint-hearted, as related by George A. Smith:

My father had been for several years very feeble in health, and for about six months previous to his baptism had not been able to visit his barn. His neighbors all believed that baptism would kill him. I cut the ice in the creek and broke a road for forty rods through the crust on two feet of snow, and the day was very cold. The neighbors looked on with astonishment, expecting to see him die in the water, but his health continued improving from that moment. That night he had a vision of the Savior entering his room and looking upon him with a smile. The next day he visited his barn. He commenced traveling and preaching through the country—his former Christian friends denouncing him as crazy, saying that the improved condition of his health was the result of insanity, and were greatly surprised that a crazy man should know more about the Bible than they did.[230]

Whether pre- or post-Mormon days, John Smith made his own decisions and exercised the moral courage to tell the truth as he understood it.

An overview of John's life is an insight into the quality of his history. The best summary is fortunately early and based on direct information from family and associates. This is his 1854 obituary, and its full biographical portions follow:

John Smith, Patriarch of the Church of Jesus Christ of Latter Day Saints, after a severe illness of one month, died at his residence in this city at 10 minutes past 11 o'clock, p.m., on the 23d inst.

Father Smith was born in Derryfield (now Manchester), [Hillsborough] County, New Hampshire, on the [16]th of July, A.D. 1781, and was baptized into the faith, which has so long preserved his life in usefulness, on the 9th of January [1832], and ordained an elder, after having been given up by the doctors to die of consumption. The weather was so cold that the ice had to be cut, and from that time he gained health and strength.

In 1833 he moved to Kirtland, Ohio, and in 1838 to Far West, Caldwell County, Missouri, and thence to Adam-ondi-Ahman, in Daviess County, where he presided over that branch of the church until expelled by the mob in 1839, and arrived in Illinois on the 28th of February of that year. He located at Green Plains, six miles from Warsaw, where he put in a crop of corn, split rails, and performed much hard labor unsuited to his health and years but obliged to be done for the support of his family. In June he moved to Commerce (since Nauvoo) and on the 4th of October was appointed to preside over the church in Iowa, and on the 12th moved to Lee County to fulfil that mission.

October 1843 he moved to Macedonia, Hancock County, Illinois, having been appointed to preside over the Saints in that place. In January 1844 he was ordained a Patriarch, and in November of that year was driven by mobbers from Macedonia to Nauvoo, where he continued to administer patriarchal blessings to the joy of thousands until the 9th of February, 1846, when he was compelled by the mob violence of the free and sovereign State of Illinois to again leave his home and cross the Mississippi with his family in search of a peaceful location, far-off, mid savages and deserts in the valleys of the mountains.

After passing a dreary winter on the right bank of the Missouri at a place called Winter Quarters, he again took up the weary ox train march on the 9th of June, 1847, and reached this place Sept. 23d, where he presided over the church in the mountains until Jan. 1st, 1849, when he was ordained Patriarch over the Church under the hands of Presidents Brigham Young and Heber C. Kimball.

He moved out of the fort on to his city lot February 1849, and this is the only spot on which he has been privileged to cultivate a garden two years in succession for the last 23 years.

In addition to a vast amount of varied and efficient aid to thousands in the way of salvation during his long and faithful ministry, he administered 5,560 Patriarchal Blessings—which are recorded in seven large and closely written books—and has closed the arduous duties of a well-occupied probation and passed to a position of rest, where his works will nobly follow and honor him, and where he will continue his able counsels for the prosperity and welfare of Zion.[231]

All that John Smith reported firsthand or from family information is reproduced here. Omitted portions are comment on the unfairness of the Mormon expulsion from Missouri or geographical and historical digressions on New England. However, John's personal recollections of Massachusetts life are included, for they are a good test of his memory after moving away at ten. For instance, he remembers the marsh haying near Ipswich, with the six-to eight-inch grass appearing at low tide:

> We have to cut and rake and carry it to a flat-bottomed boat, and when the tide rises, float it to some convenient place where it can be taken care of. This has to be attended to by night or day, according to the motion of the water.

Such older practices became unprofitable, but they were later described precisely as John Smith remembered them:

> All the grass had to be gathered at low water, and flat hayboats called "gundelows" or "gondolas" were used to carry it to the shore. . . . The thatch cutters must go with the tide regardless of the time, day or night, for they always quoted that "the tide waits for no man."[232]

Thus forty years had not impaired his memory. This is merely one example of the clear pattern of responsible accuracy in John Smith's history. His record is deficient mainly in the few sentences devoted to family backgrounds where he confessed lack of knowledge.

The sketch reproduced here is what John Smith personally entered in his diary in 1839, apparently never carrying it beyond the move to Vermont. It is fairly well written for a private narrative, and but slight editing has been done, brackets indicating any additions or changes.[233] Toward the end of his life in Utah, the patriarch dictated his life history again, at "the request of my son John." However, the "few incidents of my life for the benefit of my children and friends" were a virtual repetition of the 1839 memoir.[234] Any significant deviation in the 1851 account is noted, but it differs mainly in shortening some events. The account reproduced here is more vigorous and informative, partly due

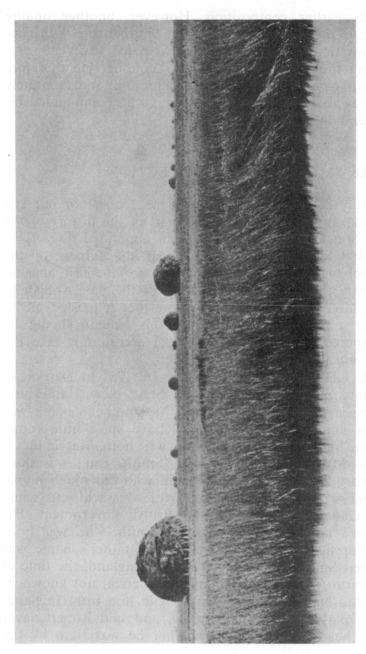

HAY MARSHES NEAR IPSWICH, MASSACHUSETTS

to its earlier composition. However, another quality appears in its introduction. John Smith wrote with conviction that his family had participated in events preparing the world for the Lord's coming. He therefore felt obligated to sketch their background, and accurately portray the character of his father, who commanded his admiration.

JOHN SMITH'S 1839 RECOLLECTIONS

July 20, 1839. This day by the request of our son [I] take my pen to write some part of the history of my life. Son George Albert has been appointed one of the Twelve Special Witnesses to bear the fulness of the gospel to the nations of the earth for the last time, to prepare the way for the coming of the Son Ahman in his glory.[235] On his leaving home [he] requested me to make a record of our lives for his benefit, should he be spared till after my decease. I accordingly take my pen and proceed as follows:

I, John Smith, was born July 16, 1781 in Derryfield, County of [Hillsborough], and State New Hampshire, where my father then resided. My mother's name was Mary Duty. Of her parentage I have but a little knowledge. My father, Asael Smith, was born March the 7, 1744. My grandfather, Samuel Smith, Esq., was born January 26, 1714. He was a man who did much public business in the Commonwealth of Massachusetts while the colonies were under the British government. His father's name was also Samuel Smith, who was born in Topsfield January 26, 1666. His father's name was Robert Smith, who came from old England, the time of his birth (neither his landing in America) not known.[236] He had one brother who came with him from England. They parted soon after landing, and said Robert never after heard of him. And whether he was slain by the

Indians or settled in some other part of the colonies and was instrumental of bringing forth some part of the great number who bear the name of Smith in America is unknown.

My parents had eleven children. Their names were Jesse, the first; Priscilla, second; Joseph, third; Asael, fourth; Mary, fifth; Samuel, sixth; Silas, seventh; John, eighth, Susan, ninth; Stephen, tenth; Sarah, the eleventh.[237] My father had one brother, who lived with my grandfather. His name was Samuel. He had thirteen children, but only two sons that survived to the age of manhood, viz., Jacob and Jabez. In what part of the land they or their child[ren] dwell I know not.

My grandfather died when I [was] quite young. I remember my father's returning home from Massachusetts, where he had been to visit his father in his last sickness. I well remember how melancholy he appeared when he called his children round him and told us that our grandfather was dead.

My grandfather [had] a great deal of public business to attend, which occupied his time so much that he had left his own affairs in a condition very difficult to settle by anyone but himself.[238] My uncle Samuel, who lived with my grandfather at the time of his death, after finding the condition his estate was in, came to New Hampshire to counsel with my father on the subject. He said it was not possible to pay the debts with the property that was left under the then existing circumstances. My father not being so well acquainted with the state of affairs as his elder brother Samuel, thought that it might be done. "For," said he, "I am not willing that my father, who has done so much business, should have it said of him that he died insolvent." And [he] urged hard to have my uncle go on and settle the business, and he felt that the Lord would prosper him in the undertaking. But my uncle said that he had a large family and but very little property, and he could not undertake such a work without the means to do with. My father was then in low circumstances, had been in a low state of health, entirely unable to labor for three years, during which time he was only able to keep the town record, as he had held the office of town clerk for many years. He owned a small farm in Derryfield, on Merrimack River, a large and growing family, and in consequence of his late sickness [they were] in a very destitute condition. "Notwithstanding all my embarrassments," said my father, "I will undertake to settle my father's estate and save his name from going down to posterity as an insolvent debtor."

Such a thing was thought more of in those days than in this wicked generation. . . . The laws are now indeed good, but men that administer them are very vile. The just are turned out for a thing of naught, etc. Mobocracy prevails to an alarming degree, as I shall show hereafter. O Lord, enable me to guide my pen in wisdom.

But to return. I said, father was willing to manage the concerns of the estate of his deceased parent, feeling under some obligation to take care of his stepmother on account of some conversation that took place between him and his father, just before his death. The old man (for he was 72 years old) was in a state of derangement at times. He jumped out of his bed and said he must go to mill, for my family will suffer. My father replied, "I will go to mill; I will take care of the family. Dear sir, do go to bed." "Asael said he will take care of my wife."[239] Says he, "I will." To use my father's own words: "He lay down quietly, knowing that I always did as I agreed, and soon after fell asleep and was gathered to his people. This promise cost me much money and trouble, but I never regretted it. I have done as I promised." I had to mention that my father's own mother died at the time of his birth, and [he]

was brought [up] by his stepmother, "who," he says,
"did not treat him so kindly as some mothers treat their
children."

After considerable conversation with my uncle,
[they] agreed to change places. Accordingly, my father
moved his family to Topsfield, Massachusetts, and attend[ed] to the business above mentioned. I was then
in the fifth year of my age. Many things in those days
that transpired are now fresh in my memory. This I
think [was] in the spring of 1786. . . .

I now proceed with [the] record. Topsfield is a
pleasant town lying on the great turnpike road leading
from Newburyport to Boston and nine miles from Salem,
where the Puritans first settled in 1630, and is now the
second town in the state and I believe in New England.
The land for many miles about Boston and Salem is cultivated like a garden to supply the market with vege-
tables, etc. Here my father struggled hard for about
five years and made out to support his family comfortably. His stepmother was on his hands during this
time, who was sometimes rather childish. However, by
prudence and industry he had paid some part of his
father's debts. My father had been a soldier for a season
(how long [I] know not) in the war of '76—had lost
considerable in the downfall of Continental paper.[240]
This with other losses, after his old mother received her
third, [and] after supporting a large family with the scanty
means which was at his command, he could not pay the
old debts which were crowding upon him. People showed
no lenity, notwithstanding they knew that if he had not
have come forward to pay them, they never could have
got one-eighth part of what they [were] now determined
to have. He finally sold the farm for what he could get
with the encumbrance of the old lady's third on it. The
old lady appointed a nephew of hers (as she never had
any children of her own) to attend to her business, by
the name of Bigsbee.[241] With him my father agreed that

whatever the rent of her third [should] come short of her support, he would make up to her in things that she would stand a need of. He then paid all the debts that [were] against the estate and left himself almost destitute of means to support his family.

He then hired in Ipswich a farm with considerable of a stock of cows, [and] as my mother was a first-rate dairy woman, [he] moved his family on to his hired farm in the spring I.think of 1791. After setting the farm in order and giving his boys to understand what they must do, he with my oldest brother Jesse took a journey up into what was called the new state, Vermont, to seek a place to locate his family at some future time when circumstances would permit.

Ipswich was a flourishing town and a place of considerable trade—lies east from Topsfield I think about eight miles, lying on a river of the same name near where it falls into Ipswich Bay. The public buildings were an elegant court house, a jail and two meeting houses. There were six men in this jail this summer for stealing, etc. They had their trials, [were] sentenced to sit upon the gallows from one to three hours with ropes round their necks (the ropes to be from three to six or eight feet, according to their crimes)—then to be tied to the post erected for that purpose and publicly whipped with a cat-o'-nine tails from 15 to 40 lashes, as the case may be, and then [were] sentenced to hard labor on Castle Island from one to three years. This island lies three miles from Boston, where convicts used to be confined making nails and other business as the government directs. I witnessed this exhibition, the first and only one of the kind that I ever saw. I was then about ten years of age. To see men thus exposed to public view and whipped upon the naked back with such a curious whip is a thing that I have not forgotten. The cat-o'-nine-tails is a whip with nine lashes. This, the only one that I ever saw, had a staff of perhaps three feet long, curiously made and painted with different colors. The lashes were twisted very hard and painted green. I thought at that time it would be a pretty thing for a boy to play with but rather cruel to the naked back.

This season I enjoyed myself as well as I ever did in my early days. Fruit was plenty. Plum Island was in plain sight. We could see vessels riding upon the ocean daily. In haying season we used to go on to the marshes to cut and secure salt hay for stock in winter. There are places of low land about the ocean where the water usually overflows at high tide. The grass on these marshes is generally six or eight inches tall and round like a wire. We have to cut and rake and carry it to a flat-bottomed boat, and when the tide rises, float it to some convenient place where it can be taken care of.[242] This has to be attended to by night or day, according to the motion of the water. All the farmers for many miles distant from these marshes make great account of saving some of this hay for their cattle. I never heard, until my father went into the state of Vermont, that cattle would eat dry salt. . . .

To proceed, at length my father and brother returned from Vermont [and] had bought 183 acres of land; if my memory serves right, paid one dollar per acre. Jesse was then for himself and about to be married. My father gave him 50 acres of land. He, Jesse, returned with Joseph, my next oldest brother, to Vermont to cut away the timber and make preparation for the family to move on—as they then expected—the next spring. (The eastern country is all, or was, covered with heavy timber, very thick, and large trees all over the land.) However, my father changed his mind, as he could not bear to have his boys so far from him, as he always loved to have his children close by. He sold his crops on the ground and settled his affairs and set off with family for the new state in the month of October, a journey of 140 miles, thought to be in those days a monstrous long tour. Many of the people thought that it would be marvelous if ever they lived to get there. So frightened were the old lady's connections that they stirred up the nephew, Mr. Bigsbee, to take an attachment and seized upon my father's loading and teams to secure the support of the old step-mother on what might be lacking of the rent of her land, which brought my father considerable expense and trouble. However, [he] left some property with her to secure the demand and proceeded on the journey under rather unfavorable circumstances.

It is through a new country and the roads very bad, the loads heavy. Of course [we] got along very slow— [were] on the road I think 14 days passing through New Hampshire, my native state. . . .[243]

But to my record. During the time we were on the road, but little transpired worthy of note. My brother Asael drove my father's team. He had hired a man by the name of Webster, with three yoke of oxen and wagon. The second or third day we meet with my brother Joseph, who by some accident had partly fractured the bone of his leg and was on the way home, expecting the family to stay at Ipswich through the approaching winter. However, he turned back with us to Vermont. Here my father took his family, went into the woods some distance from any settlement, cut his road and made bridges, and came to the little cabin that my brothers had built for their own accomodation while to work on the land. It was loosely built after the mode of building log huts, say, 14 feet by 10. The covering was the bark of the elm, which was very plenty in that part.

My brother Jesse soon returned to Massachusetts. My oldest sister had tarried there to take care of an old aunt who was then sick with a consumption. She was my father's sister. Her husband's name was Kimball.

She had borne him a large family of children, I think
twelve, which all but two had died with the same disease
and mostly after they were men and women grown.

CHAPTER 8

Epilogue

Good history goes beyond dates, places, and external events. These are flesh and bones, but the historian also explores the world within his personalities to understand their thinking. This can be done with accuracy for both of Joseph Smith's grandfathers, since they recorded their inner convictions. Their children also wrote about the ideals of their homes, and these writings of parents and children furnish a consistent and convincing picture of an environment where honesty counted for everything. Joseph Smith's grandparents weighed their words and kept their promises in the practical world. Nor did they lightly claim religious conviction. They paid the price of intense inquiry, and candidly reported the result as they experienced it. One would not expect anything different from their prophet-grandson.

The last family gathering with a grandparent is symbolic—Mary Duty Smith "surrounded by her four sons . . . as well as several of her grandsons, upwards of six feet in height." This photograph of several generations illustrates a heritage, for striking physical resemblances imply continuities of character. Joseph Smith was like both grandfathers in patriotism, social concern, industry, personal initiative, physical courage, indomitable will, loyalty to parents, tenderness to family, reliance on the Bible, and religious convictions so deep that he was impelled to share them with others.

Joseph Smith's traits are found among New Englanders of his time, but investigation shows that his family had Yankee roots of a specific type. The Prophet's grandparents quite avoided the narrow prejudices that Parkman associated with the rural New England of the eighteenth century, but they display admirably "its combative energy, and rugged, unconquerable strength."[244]

If Joseph Smith's heritage included the commendable qualities just named, did the Smiths and Macks instill in their youth the moral capacity represented by the John Adams family? The strengths and weaknesses of that legacy have been pointedly described:

> As true New Englanders, they believed firmly in a positive life, in the full exercise of their mental powers, and the full control of their "appetites". . . . Duty, determination, integrity, self-examination—these were their guides to conduct. And if this vigorous code occasionally produced unpleasant by-products—if, for example, they were accused of being intractable, ill-mannered, irascible—it did not matter; they were true to their God, their country and themselves, and no man, they felt, could demand of them more. In short, they were earnest, certain men, capable for better or worse, of instilling in a child firm beliefs and positive standards.[245]

In a social class less on display, the grandfathers of Joseph Smith lived lives equally dedicated to uncompromising principle. Their deepest wishes concerned transmitting this to their grandchildren. Solomon Mack wrote with sincere concern that "the rising generation" be given Godly instruction: "Parents, a little caution how to train up your children in the sight of the Lord. . . . Set good examples in word, deed, and action." Similarly, Asael Smith insisted that "absolute truth" should govern his children, who should then lead their children: "Make it your chiefest work to bring them up in the ways of virtue." Joseph Smith was unquestionably exposed to an enduring moral heritage.

Victor Hugo reportedly said, "If you would civilize a man, begin with his grandmother." Both Mary Duty and Lydia Gates combined practical industry with deep spirituality. Personally loving, both were convinced, as were their husbands, that immortality was certain. These individuals are one identifiable source of the seeking faith and outgoing love that characterized Joseph Smith's parents. Love is awareness, the quality that keeps commitment from becoming fanaticism. Another safeguard on belief is humility. Asael Smith stated crisply what Solomon Mack says indirectly—hoping that death would obliterate his faults but leave "my virtues, if ever I had any, to revive and live in you." Humanity might be perfected in a few generations if that were possible. Yet Asael's hope shows his sincere desire to morally upgrade his family, though he was acutely aware of his own imperfections.

Biography, like history, has many dimensions. Is the story of a man his political offices, his bank account, or his personal growth? In the last regard Asael Smith and Solomon Mack were significant individuals. Both were energetically progressive in their own convictions and actions. Solomon's conversion came in 1810-11, but that really climaxed a lifetime of seeking. Regretting that he was not taught "common morality" by his exploiting master, Solomon exhibited uncommon morality in the ultimate relationships of loyalty and integrity. One remembers that his grandson preferred a just man who "swears a stream as long as my arm" rather than the "long, smooth-faced hypocrite."[246] Solomon confessed to Sabbath-breaking, ignoring the scriptures, swearing, and experimenting with drinking. But he is not a very convincing sinner, for he early "reflected a little on such conduct, resolving to amend from such practices." Despite his disclaimer of lapsing into worldly ways, he long had his eye on heaven. "Through the early part of my life," he had accepted the "universal principle"—that God loved all and would save all. Thus he worked within the framework of his Christian culture and Lydia Gates Mack's Christian home. If Solomon did not know chapter and verse, he well knew the message of the Lord when he later sought reassurance. But long before, he was "almost a Christian," even administering comfort to "a sick man on his death bed."[247] In his fashion Solomon was a man of faith, a faith defined clearly in the perspective of elderly years. Just as Solomon stood for principle in a worldly environment, so did Asael Smith stand for a broader Christianity in the society of narrow Calvinism. He thought secular and religious history would culminate in bursting the shackles from every form of enslavement. Two generations later a New England minister found Asael Smith's correspondence and concluded: "It is quite evident that these Smiths were possessed of a good share of respectability, intelligence, and energy of character."[248]

Glaring faults are absent from the Prophet's heritage. The most apparent defect would be an excess of generosity—which brought Solomon Mack to financial grief in signing as surety for others, or which plunged Asael Smith into years of labor for his unbreakable promise to his father. Yet true concern for others is an awesome quality, whatever its form. Asael's firm loyalty to his family is close to Solomon's dangerous pause in battle to save another's life. Selflessness is the foundation of honesty, a form of concern for the effect of one's conduct on others. Dishonesty in religious matters is hypocrisy, and both Asael Smith and Solomon Mack stood far above that. Asael's independence and skepticism of orthodoxy evidently influenced his grandson more than a little. Solomon also stood outside religious conformity for a lifetime, only to be spiritually converted to Christ after applying Asael's double tools, scripture and reason. Both had experienced spiritual promptings; yet both were too practical to be categorized as mystics. Just as they stood for fair dealing in everyday affairs, their religious sincerity cannot be challenged. And the wives are as spiritually genuine as their husbands. This is the critical relevance of the grandparents for understanding Joseph Smith, Jr.

History hardly possesses tools to prove or disprove

any revelation from God, but it can assess the character of those who claim visions. Three generations of Smiths emerge: capable grandparents who valued "virtue" above all else; parents whose home life maintained this moral inheritance;[249] and a prophet-grandson whose youth was marked by the honesty of his heritage—years are compressed into his brother's simple verdict, "Joseph was a truthful boy."[250] Yet he had a quick mind, including the ready wit of Asael Smith, and a healthy mistrust of mere religious posing. Knowing that Joseph Smith was both truthful and astute will not convince many that he received revelation, since they will not accept the possibility. But that does not excuse historical mudslinging which mislabels family members to more easily explain away Joseph Smith. The record shows a birthright of honor and idealism. Settled family patterns are not easily altered, particularly in pioneer generations demanding close cooperation for survival. Joseph Smith's parents matured under intense exposure to moral responsibility, unselfishness, personal tenacity, intellectual awareness, and intelligent sincerity. These are not the raw materials for shaping an imposter or fanatic.

Notes on Text

The lives of members of Joseph Smith's family have been reconstructed from hundreds of sources. Evidence for the narrative appears here, together with commentary on historical problems. References to other notes are frequent—but all cross-references are to notes in this section, not notes in any source cited. Titles are listed with full publication data when first cited, and shortened if often repeated. In the latter case the full citation is alphabetized in the bibliography.

[1]"History of Joseph Smith," *Times and Seasons,* vol. 3 (1842), p. 727; the later prologue quote on rumor is found ibid., p. 772. The more convenient reprint is Joseph Smith, *History of the Church of Jesus Christ of Latter-day Saints* (Salt Lake City, 1902), vol. 1, p. 1, with the later prologue quote on p. 19.

[2]Journal of Joseph Smith, kept by Willard Richards, July 9, 1843, also cit. Joseph Smith, *History,* vol. 5, p. 498. The full quotation is the epigraph of this book on p. xix.

[3]Solomon Mack, *A Narrative of the Life of Solomon Mack* (Windsor, Vt. [1811]), p. 3. Citation will not follow the erroneous *Narraitve,* which is incorrectly spelled on all known copies, modifying Marcus A. McCorison, *Vermont Imprints, 1778-1820* (Worcester, Mass., 1963), p. 252. Although Mack's pamphlet is regularly dated 1810, he gave no time of publication, and it apparently was printed after the winter of 1810-11, since it describes conversion at that time. He was converted "in my seventy-sixth year" (p. 25), which by his understanding of his birthdate would run from Sept. 26, 1810, to Sept. 26, 1811 (p. 3). The sickness that precipitated his conversion came in the fall of 1810, but the conversion was toward spring of 1811: "In the fall of the year 1810, in the 76th year of my age, I was taken with the rheumatism, and confined me all winter" (p. 18). "All the winter I was laid up with the rheumatism . . . but in the spring the Lord appeared to be with me" (p. 23). "I called upon the Lord the greatest part of the winter, and towards spring . . . light shined into my soul" (ibid.).

So the pamphlet must be dated no earlier than 1811, and it was probably written immediately after conversion, since no events later than the spring of 1811 are mentioned. Lucy Smith's preliminary manuscript mentions the work as "written by my father in the 80th year of his age," but this may be a general recollection. The *Narrative* mentions his first crippling accident "34 years ago" (p. 11) and then implies a very long recovery before he went to sea privateering. As discussed later (n. 42), a newspaper reports a battle in which he participated in 1779. If he wrote his *Narrative* in 1811, then the accident 34 years before that would be 1777, which matches his facts of some recovery time before the 1779 privateering.

[4]For an abstract of land transactions in the years 1729 to 1731, see Archibald F. Bennett, "Solomon Mack and His Family," *Improvement Era*, vol. 58 (Sept. 1955), p. 631. The will of John Mack is copied by Sophia Martin, *Mack Genealogy: The Descendants of John Mack of Lyme, Conn.* (Rutland, Vt., 1903), vol. 1, pp. 18-21. John gave Ebenezer "my house and barn and orchard and all my lands in Lyme . . . not already disposed of," together with "the remainder of my movable estate."

[5]Lucy Smith, *Biographical Sketches of Joseph Smith* (Liverpool, 1853), p. 15.

[6]Mack, *Narrative*, p. 3.

[7]Ibid. Solomon gives his age of being bound out as four, but he was possibly seven, since he dates his birth three years late, as discussed in n. 10.

[8]Ibid., p. 4.

[9]Louis Kaplan, *A Bibliography of American Autobiographies* (Madison, Wis., 1962), p. 188.

[10]Mack, *Narrative*, p. 5. Although Lucy Mack Smith and Solomon Mack give his birthdate as Sept. 26, 1735, the vital records of Lyme, Conn., give Solomon's birth as Sept. 15, 1732. As Archibald Bennett suggested, the master may have misrepresented Solomon's age to him in order to prolong his service. Connecticut Vital Records Index.

[11]Mack, *Narrative*, p. 47. Colonial records show that he enlisted under Capt. James Harris Sept. 10 and was discharged Nov. 24, 1755; at Ft. Edward he reenlisted under Capt. Israel Putnam Nov. 24, 1755, and was discharged May 29, 1756. *Rolls of Connecticut*

Men in the French and Indian War, 1755-1762, Collections of the Connecticut Historical Society, vol. 9 (1903), pp. 44, 79.

[12]Mack, *Narrative,* p. 6.

[13]Ibid.

[14]Lucy Smith, *Biographical Sketches,* p. 108.

[15]Mack, *Narrative,* p. 7.

[16]Fortification height is given in the *Journals of Major Robert Rogers* (London, 1765), p. 116.

[17]Francis Parkman, citing an officer-participant, *Montcalm and Wolfe* (reprint; New York, 1962), p. 422.

[18]Mack, *Narrative,* p. 7.

[19]Ibid., p. 8. Mack was obviously in Putnam's company, since Putnam led out, and Solomon "was in the front" of the march. Incidentally, a good history finds that Solomon Mack gave the most useful description of the initial assault. John R. Cuneo, *Robert Rogers of the Rangers* (New York, 1959), p. 89.

[20]"The Narrative of Major Thompson Maxwell," *Historical Collections of the Essex Institute,* vol. 7 (1865), p. 100. Although the recollection inverts the sequence of the assault on Ticonderoga and the ambush, personal details must be accurate.

[21]Mack, *Narrative,* p. 8.

[22]*Journals of Major Robert Rogers* (London, 1765), p. 118.

[23]Mack's exploits during the Ticonderoga campaign of 1758 ring true. He relates them conservatively, and their factual structure is exact. They are introduced with, "soon after I enlisted under Major Spencer in 1758, and went over the lakes" (*Narrative,* p. 7). Solomon Mack appears on the muster roll of Major Joseph Spencer's company, with enlistment date June 5, 1758, and discharge Nov. 18, 1758. Incidentally, Solomon mentions Gershom "Bowley" (probably a typographical error) and Ensign Worcester on the field during the ambush. Gershom Rowley appears on the muster roll in Mack's unit, and Ensign Peter Wooster is named in an adjoining company. *Rolls of Connecticut Men in the French and Indian War, 1755-1762, Collections of the Connecticut Historical Society,* vol. 10 (1905), pp. 34-37.

[24]Mack, *Narrative,* p. 9. This episode shows how far Solomon Mack developed in his life, since he mentions that he did not then

know "how to write or read to any amount what others had written or printed." His autobiography later displays some skill in composition.

The "two years" at Crown Point as a sutler is to be preferred over the "27 years" of the errata (p. 47), an obvious typographical error. The marriage date is given by Solomon as 1759 (*Narrative,* p. 47, correcting p. 9). This is confirmed in the Connecticut Vital Records Index (Lyme): "Gates, Lydia, of East Haddam, d. Dan[ie]ll, of East Haddam, m. Solomon Mack, of Lyme, Jan. 4, 1759." Cp. the record of the Second Congregational Church of East Haddam (Millington), Conn., vol. 1, p. 47: "January 4, 1759: Solomon Mack, of Lyme and Lidya Gates."

Lucy Smith quotes her father on the time of courtship in *Biographical Sketches,* p. 18, and her preliminary manuscript slightly varies the phraseology, indicating that "I was shortly united" to Lydia Gates after becoming acquainted.

[25]Mack, *Narrative,* pp. 9-12. Greater detail is given in Lucy's quotation from her father's "journal" (cp. n. 29), *Biographical Sketches,* p. 18: "Having received a large amount of money for my services in the army, and deeming it prudent to make an investment of the same in real estate, I contracted for the whole town of Granville, in the state of New York. On the execution of the deed, I paid all the money that was required in the stipulation, which stipulation also called for the building of a number of log houses. I accordingly went to work to fulfil this part of the contract, but after laboring a short time, I had the misfortune to cut my leg, which subjected me during that season to the care of the physician. I hired a man to do the work, and paid him in advance in order to fulfil my part of the contract, but he ran away. with the money without performing the labor, and the consequence was, I lost the land altogether."

[26]Mack, *Narrative,* p. 10.

[27]Lyme, Conn., Land Records, vol. 9, p. 505, records Solomon Mack's purchase of a tract of land and house in Lyme on Oct. 18, 1756, for 80 pounds. Location of Solomon's land is generally specified "in the North Society of said Lyme." Ibid., vol. 10, pp. 153, 385; vol. 11, pp. 29, 79; vol. 13, p. 410.

[28]Deeds are abstracted in Bennett, "Solomon Mack," vol. 58, pp. 713-14. Probably because of his holdings and roots in Lyme, that is given as his residence in the deeds after he had moved away.

[29]Solomon Mack, cit. Lucy Smith, *Biographical Sketches,* p. 19, where the date of moving to Marlow is given and the birth of four

children there (cp. n. 86). The daughter quotes from "a sketch of my father's life, written by himself" (p. 15), which she calls "my father's journal" (p. 20), a term also employed by Solomon of his own pamphlet (*Narrative,* p. 44). Lucy's preliminary manuscript indicates that her "extracts" are from "an old document which I have in my possession written by my father." Lucy probably had a manuscript draft with certain incidents not in Solomon's published pamphlet. The details of the Marlow stay are only given by her. Cp. n. 43 and n. 44.

[30]See Records of Marlow, N. H., State Copy, vol. 1, p. 38 (purchase of May 15, 1767), pp. 344-45 (Mar. 10, 1767, election). For the office of "deer reeve" in the general area, see Sylvester Judd, *History of Hadley* (Northampton, Mass., 1863), p. 357.

[31]Records of Marlow, N. H., State Copy, vol. 1, p. 90 (Dec. 8, 1770). Town records have a number of references to Solomon Mack's land from 1767 through 1773; see pp. 22, 69, 72, 89, 107, 125, 158.

[32]Chesire County, N. H., Land Records, vol. 2, p. 30 (Mar. 25, 1773). Solomon Mack resided in Marlow during 1771, signing a petition there as one of the "proprietors by purchase," and also during 1772, when he and his brother Elisha are enumerated as heads of families on Jan. 7, 1772. Nathaniel Bouton (ed.), *Town Papers Relating to Towns in New Hampshire,* State Papers Series, vol. 9 (Concord, N. H., 1875), pp. 546-58.

[33]Mack, *Narrative,* p. 11. Elisha last held the mill property in 1784, when it briefly passed through the hands of Solomon's son Jason. Cheshire Co., N. H., Land Records, vol. 8, pp. 617-18; Vol. 9, pp. 85-86, 331-32. For the responsible tradition of Solomon's participation in the mill enterprise, see Silvanus Hayward, *History of the Town of Gilsum, New Hampshire* (Manchester, N. H., 1881), p. 204, which also identifies the location in the lower village, "where the Stone Bridge now stands." Cp. p. 136, which indicates the first gristmill as "built by Elisha Mack and his brother Solomon about 1776, near the Stone Bridge." Probably Solomon's grandson at Gilsum was one source of such information (n. 79).

[34]Mack, *Narrative,* p. 10. Gunpowder shortages and corrective measures are outlined in Orlando W. Stephenson, "The Supply of Gunpowder in 1776," *American Historical Review,* vol. 30 (1925), p. 271 ff., with the Washington letter cited at p. 274.

[35]Mack, *Narrative,* p. 10. "Skenesborough" is an early name given to the village or city of Whitehall, N. Y., at the south end of

Lake Champlain. Horatio Gates Spafford, *Gazetteer of the State of New York* (Albany, 1824), p. 569.

[36]Mack, *Narrative*, p. 11. Since the pamphlet was probably written in 1811, this crippling accident took place about 1777, "34 years ago." Cp. n. 3.

[37]Ibid., pp. 11-12. The immediately preceding accident took place about 1777 (n. 36) and corresponds with Solomon's residence in Gilsum and the tradition of his millwork there (n. 33).

[38]Ibid., p. 17. Since one similar episode is named among outstanding afflictions, they appear to be infrequent: "at another time I fell in a fit at Tunbridge" (p. 18). None of Solomon's three passages mentioning a "fit" can be certainly equated with seizures, though the Winchester episode discussed in the text seems to be this.

It is even possible that Solomon used "fit" in the early sense of "a mortal crisis; a bodily state (whether painful or not) that betokens death." *The Oxford English Dictionary* (Oxford, 1933), vol. 4, p. 262. Although historical dictionaries call this a middle-English usage, Solomon and Lucy Mack Smith use "fit" in just this sense. When her mother almost died about 1780, she "had a severe fit of sickness," one which kept her in bed for weeks and obviously had nothing to do with any seizure. *Biographical Sketches*, p. 36. Lucy also quotes John Smith's journal in the same usage. Joseph Smith, Sr., was cautioned not to see his aged father, Asael, until morning, for he had been in critical condition—"was just recovering from a severe fit." Ibid., p. 154; cp. ibid., p. 169, where "a heavy fit of sickness" lasted "four weeks," when Emma overtaxed herself in 1830. Solomon uses the term of his own mother's extended sickness, on the initial page of his *Narrative*: "Hannah Mack departed this life in 1796 with a long fit of sickness." His description of his own boyhood sickness is similar, where an accident produced leg infection "that terminated in a severe fit of sickness" (ibid., p. 5).

[39]The major statement of this theory is I. Woodbridge Riley, *The Founder of Mormonism, A Psychological Study of Joseph Smith, Jr.* (New York, 1902).

[40]For the assumptions behind the theory, see ibid., p. 345. Admitting that "the diagnosis of an apparent epilepsy in Smith's visionary seizures is difficult," the author nevertheless is certain that Solomon Mack proves his point: "But the prognosis is assured from the antecedents of the patient. . . . Foremost is heredity." Ac-

tual evidence of any hereditary disorder is completely absent in Solomon's case.

[41]See, e. g., ibid., p. 15, where the author refers to "the 'visions and revelations' and other abnormalities of grandfather and grandson alike."

[42]*The Connecticut Gazette and the Universal Intelligencer,* Mar. 25, 1779. I am indebted to Doris E. Cook at the Connecticut Historical Society for locating the article, and to Mrs. Elizabeth B. Knox of the New London County Historical Society for furnishing the leads for finding it. Solomon Mack is accurate in describing the *Beaver* as 114 tons, with about 80 aboard, commanded by Capt. Havens. The commission and bond filed Sept. 3, 1779, describes the *Beaver:* Connecticut sloop. Guns: 12. Crew: 65. Bond: $5,000. Master: William Havens." *Naval Records of the American Revolution, 1775-1788* (Washington, 1906), p. 233. Further details on the *Beaver* are given by Louis F. Middlebrook, *History of Maritime Connecticut During the American Revolution, 1775-1783* (Salem, Mass., 1925), vol. 2, pp. 54-57: (1) Capt. Havens commanded the *Beaver* under an earlier commission and bond from late 1778; (2) The *Beaver* had a very active record of service, capturing eight British ships during April to June 1779, when Solomon Mack was probably on board; (3) The dangers of privateering are underlined by the *Beaver's* capture by British warships on Mar. 22, 1781; (4) Admirality Court records describe the captured ship as follows: "the said sloop *Beaver* is of the burthen of about one hundred and ten tons—that there were eighty men on board the same (officers included) at the time she was taken."

[43]Lucy Smith, preliminary manuscript, in which the section on Jason is more detailed, and placed in first person as quoted from Solomon. *Biographical Sketches* places the episode in third person, but its origin is evidently the fuller version of Solomon's autobiography (cp. n. 29). Note that Liverpool is located between Halifax and the Bay of Fundy. Mack, *Narrative,* pp. 15-16. For the possible source of the money, cp. n. 46.

[44]Lucy Smith, preliminary manuscript, evidently citing Solomon's fuller version (cp. n. 29). The quoted passage is preceded by the following (neither of which are in *Biographical Sketches,* which uses the third person here): "But whither he has fled or what his fate has been, God knows. Tis long since he left us, and I fear my grey hairs will go down in sorrow to grave else I shall see his face."

Since Jason visited in Tunbridge when both Lucy and Solomon lived there, this quotation possibly indicates an earlier journal entry. Solomon might have kept a personal history at different times, in addition to the composition of his printed autobiography in 1811. Cp. n. 29. On Jason's absence, see n. 51.

[45]Solomon Mack indicates that he "sailed up the Bay of Fundy and wintered at Hawton." Although no "Hawton" can be located, Horton (and the present Horton Landing) is on the Minas Basin, at the head of the Bay of Fundy. ("Hawton" is evidently a phonetic spelling of one Northeast pronunciation of Horton.) Simeon Perkins' diary (cit. n. 46) mentions travelers from Horton village, which was the "social and business centre of the township of Horton" in the eighteenth century, though it later lost ground to neighboring Wolfville and Kentville. Arthur W. H. Eaton, *History of Kings County, Nova Scotia* (Salem, Mass., 1910), p. 123. Solomon's wintering there and contracting to take 30 passengers to New London fit the picture of early settlement of Horton by numerous eastern Connecticut families. Ibid., p. 69-72. Cp. Jean Stephenson, "The Connecticut Settlement of Nova Scotia Prior to the Revolution," *Special Aids to Genealogical Research in Northeastern and Central States*, Special Publications of the National Genealogical Society, No. 16 (Washington, D.C., 1962), p. 5, which mentions the active shipping trade between Horton and Connecticut.

[46]D. C. Harvey and C. Bruce Fergusson (eds.), *The Diary of Simeon Perkins, 1780-1789, Publications of the Champlain Society*, vol. 36 (Toronto, 1958), p. 372. Simeon Perkins frequently mentions members of the family of Samuel Mack (1737-83), who settled near Port Medway, ten miles east of Liverpool. Samuel Mack was Solomon's brother. Born Nov. 15, 1736, he married Lydia Brainerd Feb. 14, 1758, and the couple had children, Lydia (b. Nov. 10, 1758, m. Nathaniel Spencer, Apr. 16, 1778 at Chatham, Conn.) and Abigail (b. Apr. 10, 1760). Connecticut Vital Records Index; cp. Martin, *Mack Genealogy*, vol. 1, pp. 881-82, which gives proper dates of the foregoing, but erroneous information regarding Samuel's remaining in New England. Birth and marriage certificates of these daughters appear in the probate file of Samuel Mack, one signed at Chatham, Conn., mentioning that Lydia is "the daughter of . . . Samuel Mack, late of Liverpool in Nova Scotia." Probate Records, Queens County, Liverpool, N. S., File A 352. Samuel had remarried in Liverpool on Sept. 25, 1766, to Desire Cahoon, and two sons had names corresponding to the sons of Solomon Mack

(Stephen, b. 1771, and Solomon, b. 1774). "Marriages, Births and Deaths," typescript copy of Vital Records Book at Liverpool, N. S., p. 13. Dr. C. Bruce Fergusson, Provincial Archivist of Nova Scotia, has kindly furnished (from T. B. Smith's genealogical notes) the Christian inscription on Samuel's tombstone: ". . . who departed this life October the 10th, 1783, aged 46 years," an age agreeing with Samuel's birthdate as recorded in Connecticut.

Samuel's death in 1783 might well be related to the money Solomon went to Liverpool to collect. Samuel's son, also Samuel, named one of his sons Jason Mack, but he was born Nov. 13, 1802. "Marriages, Births and Deaths," typescript copy of Vital Records Book at Liverpool, N. S., p. 53. Thus Solomon Mack's son Jason is the only known person who might have been involved in the 1787 shipwreck.

Perkins' mention of the grounded vessel of Jason Mack agrees with Solomon's account in time of year, location (between Halifax and Liverpool), and circumstances. Perkins apparently knew Solomon Mack's son Jason in later years also. Lucy Smith indicates that her brother later headed a cooperative settlement in New Brunswick: "Owning a schooner himself, he took their produce to Liverpool, as it was then the best market." *Biographical Sketches,* p. 52. In Perkins' diary "Mr. Jason Mack, from New Brunswick" repeatedly ships into Liverpool, and more than once his "Topsail Schooner" is mentioned. Charles Bruce Fergusson, *Diary of Simeon Perkins, 1797-1803, Publications of the Champlain Society* (Toronto, 1967), vol. 43, pp. 50, 243, 310, 333, 474.

[47]Solomon's loss and repurchase of his vessel appear in his *Narrative,* p. 16. Solomon indicates his purchase of the schooner from "Captain Foster," for whom he had previously taken fishing voyages. The Robert Fosters (Sr. and Jr.) are prominent shipowners who were also in the fishing business in and near Liverpool, as indicated in Simeon Perkins' diary.

Describing his schooner, Solomon mentions "both masts" and the storm forcing "all hands" to leave, except himself and son (pp. 14-15). A list of ships owned in Queens County June 23, 1789, includes 19 schooners, ranging from 20-ton to 64-ton capacity, with 42-ton average; cit. James F. More, *History of Queens County, N. S.* (Halifax, 1873), p. 202. Simeon Perkins built several schooners and records the dimensions of one of 48 tons as follows: "She measures 45 feet keel in the whole . . . and we allow she will be 16 feet 3 inches beam and 6 feet 5 inches hold." Harvey and Fergusson,

Diary of Simeon Perkins, vol. 36, p. 281, entry July 13, 1785. Perkins sent complements of five or six men on his schooners, including captain and mate (e. g., ibid., 342, 358).

For background on schooners, see John Robinson and George Francis Dow, *Sailing Ships of New England, 1607-1907* (Westminster, Md., 1953), pp. 25-28. Later ships generally resembling Solomon's vessel can be seen in Basil Greenhill and Ann Giffard, *The Merchant Sailing Ship: A Photographic History* (New York, 1970), pp. 49, 52, 84-85.

[48]*Narrative,* pp. 16-17, reports the end of four years at sea, and this time is copied in Lucy Smith's *Biographical Sketches.* Lucy's preliminary manuscript is more specific here, giving three years and 10 months as the total time for Jason and Solomon at sea, with two years elapsing before the forged notification of death. Cp. n. 51.

[49]The 1779 enlistment is in *Massachusetts Soldiers and Sailors in the Revolutionary War* (Boston, 1902), vol. 10, p. 109, which also includes Stephen's reenlistment at Montague in 1881. Lovisa's marriage date appears in the Montague, Mass., vital records and is discussed in chapter 4.

[50]"Narrative of the Life of Joseph Tuttle," undated typescript in possession of the Mahoning Valley Historical Society, Youngstown, Ohio, and furnished by courtesy of Mrs. Walter Scharf, Jr., director. Although the original is at present unlocated, the unusual detail of the typescript guarantees its authenticity. This copy generally agrees with the typescript preserved by the Tuttle family in Painesville, Ohio, which is followed herein. Mrs. Josephine C. Shaffer, research genealogist of Painesville, Ohio, located this copy. The Joseph Tuttle who wrote the manuscript (1796-1884) is the son of the Joseph Tuttle who was Lovisa Mack's husband (1756-1816), who died when his son was just 20. The last date mentioned in the "Narrative" is 1840, which gives a general date of composition. Comments appended at the end are by the author's son, Judge Grandison Newell Tuttle, who mentions his father's death in 1884 and alludes to the "narrative above copied." The recollections of Joseph Tuttle were clearly in existence in 1893, when sections are quoted and paraphrased in the biographies of Joseph's sons F. W. Tuttle and Judge Grandison Newell Tuttle. *Biographical History of Northeastern Ohio* (Chicago, 1893), pp. 886 and 294 ff. Since Judge Tuttle was named after a prominent critic of Joseph Smith, the Tuttles would obviously be realistic in appraising his grandfather Mack. By coincidence, the

second Joseph Tuttle (the author of the "Narrative") lived in the immediate vicinity of the Mormon gathering location, Kirtland, Ohio. His son (Judge Tuttle) reported the following episode in connection with the first Joseph Tuttle and Lovisa Mack: "Her sister was the mother of Joseph Smith, the founder of Mormonism. And after her son became distinguished as the leader of the new faith, she removed with him to Kirtland, Ohio; and learning that a son of her deceased sister's husband was living in the vicinity, tried to interest the Judge's father, who then lived in Concord, Ohio, in their family. But he had so poor an opinion of the Mormon faith that he took no interest in making an acquaintance with a family who had at one time been connected in marriage with his father." *Biographical History of Northeastern Ohio,* p. 294. Cp. n. 103 and n. 104.

On the "Narrative's" naming Sunderland as Solomon Mack's residence, this is the residence of John Tuttle, father-in-law of Lovisa Mack. However, all evidence places Solomon Mack in Montague (the adjoining town north) in the period surrounding Lovisa's marriage. Documentation on Lovisa's marriage and further Mack history of that time appear in chapter 4.

[51]Note 48 documents the nearly four-year period at sea. Since Solomon's *Narrative* reflects a free-trade era, it is unlikely that he would have begun his sea ventures before the close of the Revolutionary War, which terminated officially at the Treaty of Paris, signed Sept. 3, 1783, with ratifications exchanged between the United States and Great Britian in May 1784. At Liverpool, Nova Scotia, where Solomon first went to collect his debt, Simeon Perkins describes anti-United States privateering in the early months of 1783, shortly afterward mentioning news of the peace negotiations "and that America is to have a free trade to all parts of the British Dominions." Later that year he mentions voyages from Boston and Salem to his home of Liverpool. Harvey and Fergusson, *Diary of Simeon Perkins, 1780-1789,* vol. 36, pp. 179, 181-84, 196, 198.

One definite date in the four-year odyssey of Solomon and Jason Mack is Perkins' report of Jason Mack's stranded vessel near Liverpool, discussed in the text and n. 46. Perkins heard of this at Halifax on May 30, 1787, and Solomon worked to earn money to repurchase his schooner and engage in the coastal trade after that. Thus 1784 to 1788 seems a good approximation of his extended sea career. Solomon's brother Samuel died near Liverpool, Nova Scotia, Oct. 10, 1783, the possible event that caused Solomon's journey there (n. 46).

The foregoing analysis fits the events of the *Narrative,* pp. 16-17, describing arrangements on leaving for sea. Mack's debtor, Nathaniel Peck of Lyme, assigned a $100 debt to Mack's creditor, "John Cordy" of Lyme, only to have Peck die shortly and "Cordy" get but a fraction of the money due. The Connecticut Cemetery Index gives the death of one Nathaniel Peck of Old Lyme as Mar. 26, 1784, which fits Mack's recollections, since the Connecticut Will Index names his estate as insolvent. "Cordy's" correct name is McCordy or McCurdy (see opening of chapter 3). The inventory of Peck's creditors was filed Nov. 8, 1784, and listed a debt of 44 pounds in favor of John McCurdy. Probate Records, New London, Conn., vol. 1, p. 138.

Jason Mack was apparently still in New England when he purchased the Gilsum saw and gristmill property of his family on Aug. 11, 1784, and when he shortly sold the same property at a slight loss on Aug. 25, 1784, to "Edward Jones, of Boston . . . merchant." Cheshire Co., N. H., Land Records, vol. 8, pp. 617-18; vol. 9, pp. 331-32. Since Solomon's *Narrative* indicates the end of his nearly four-year period in the fall, perhaps these transactions had something to do with closing out interests before going to sea, possibly to secure a stable situation for his family before leaving— as hinted by the *Narrative.*

Lucy Smith (*Biographical Sketches,* p. 21) says that Jason accompanied his father on the trip to Liverpool following a romance that began "a short time" after he turned 20. He was the first child of Solomon's 1759 marriage (cp. n. 24) and therefore turned 20 about 1780. With time after that for his courtship to begin and mature, 1784 generally fits Lucy's recollections of his leaving New England for the Maritime Provinces.

[52]Hayward, *History of the Town of Gilsum,* p. 432. Although this information probably came from the family (n. 79), the inclusion of Samuel as a New England builder seems erroneous, since he lived in Nova Scotia after 1766 (n. 46). Yet he did run a sawmill there for years, and his son even wrote a pamphlet defending his rights to the mill-dam. Harvey and Fergusson, *Diary of Simeon Perkins,* vol. 36, p. 22, n. 1, and Fergusson, *Diary of Simeon Perkins,* vol. 39, p. 30, n. 2. Elsewhere in his history Hayward seems to know less about Samuel than his brothers (p. 204).

[53]Josiah Gilbert Holland, *History of Western Massachusetts* (Springfield, Mass., 1855), pp. 308-309. Holland, who serialized his history first in the *Springfield Republican,* evidently got much of his information from recollections of others. He was not born until

1819, but was a responsible newspaperman and later a prominent author. Possible sources appear in the preface: "kind correspondents in each of the one hundred towns embraced in the work have copied records, gathered statistics, and corrected mis-statements after their publication in the newspaper. By far the larger part of the work is from entirely new and original materials" (vol. 1, p. 4).

Statutes involving the company behind this project are Mass. Laws, 1791, chap. 32 (Feb. 22, 1792), *Acts and Laws of the Commonwealth of Massachusetts* (Boston, 1895); and Mass. Laws, 1792, chap. 39 (Feb. 25, 1793), ibid. For tradition on Elisha Mack at Greenfield, see Francis M. Thompson, *History of Greenfield* (Greenfield, Mass., 1904), vol. 1, pp. 532-35; vol. 2, p. 686. The act naming Elisha Mack as a bridge proprietor is Mass. Laws, 1791, chap. 46 (Mar. 6, 1792), which requires specifications of being "well built, at least twenty feet wide, of good and suitable materials and well covered with plank and timber on the top . . . with sufficient rails on each side for . . . safety."

When Elisha Mack sold his mill property in Gilsum, N. H., his conveyance makes clear his Montague residence, calling him "Elisha Mack, of Montague . . . gent[leman]." Cheshire Co., N. H., Land Records, vol. 9, pp. 85-86 (July 14, 1784); witnesses on the deed are Montague, Mass., residents Moses and Elisha Gunn. Elisha Mack was still at Montague in 1798, when the U.S. direct tax was levied there. *Vital Records of Montague, Massachuestts* (Salem, Mass., 1934), p. 162. Elisha Mack's ingenuity was proverbial. Holland mentions his leather diving suit, complete with tube for air, which (in this version) was made by a Scottish employee. Hayward's Gilsum *History* reports the same suit as worn "at the first celebration of independence at Montague, Mass." (p. 432).

[54]There is possible confusion in the records of Gilsum between father Solomon Mack and his son, Solomon Mack, Jr. This is avoided in the tax lists of 1796 and 1797, where both Solomon Mack and Solomon Mack, Jr., are enumerated. Only "Solomon Mack" appears from 1793 to 1795. However, Solomon Mack, Jr., was only 20 in 1793 (n. 89) and was not married until Aug. 27, 1797, according to Gilsum vital records; in the light of n. 55 one would assume that his father is the "Solomon Mack" taxed there from 1793 to 1795, and that on coming of age, the son is first listed separately in 1796 and 1797. He remains on the tax lists and is prominent in the town minutes from this time, and is called only Solomon Mack, since his father moved to Vermont after this time.

⁵⁵Lucy's preliminary manuscript adds facts on her early life: "From Gilsum father moved to Montague. . . . Two years before sister Lovina's death I visited sister Tuttle, who was then sick in South Hadley. . . . Before I returned home my father moved back to Gilsum, where I continued with my parents until my youngest sister's death." Since Lovina and Lovisa's deaths are discussed in chapter 4, the probable date need only be noted here as 1794. So Lucy's narrative indicates late 1792 and 1794 as Gilsum years for her family. Solomon also identifies Gilsum as his home when Lovisa died, in the *Narrative* extract reprinted in chapter 4.

⁵⁶Lydia's marriage in early 1786 is found in the Gilsum, N. H., vital records, and Samuel Bill's prominence in town affairs, including service as selectman for ten years, is found in Hayward, *History of the Town of Gilsum,* pp. 73, 128, 197, 266. Bennett summarized this information in "Solomon Mack," vol. 59, pp. 90-91.

Lucy Mack Smith's marriage in early 1796 is recorded at Tunbridge, Vt. For her parents' residence at Gilsum before and after this date, see *Biographical Sketches,* pp. 36-37, 45. Lucy's preliminary manuscript is explicit on where her parents resided when she stayed with them after living with brother Stephen in Tunbridge: "after which I made a visit to my parents in Gilsum and my uncles and aunts in Marlow." Her marriage immediately follows in this narrative, as in *Biographical Sketches.* Further history of Lucy's years before marriage is in chapter 4.

⁵⁷Mack, *Narrative,* p. 17.

⁵⁸Ibid., pp. 11, 17-18.

⁵⁹Lucy Smith, *Biographical Sketches,* p. 20. For Lucy's apparent access to a fuller manuscript of her father, see n. 29. This statement is not quoted in Lucy's preliminary manuscript.

⁶⁰Mack, *Narrative,* p. 20.

⁶¹The entire passage of Matt. 11:28-30 impressed Solomon; he twice tells the impact of the verse. *Narrative,* pp. 18-19, 21.

⁶²Ibid., pp. 22; cp. p. 19.

⁶³Ibid., pp. 23-24.

⁶⁴Ibid., p. 44.

⁶⁵Ibid., p. 25; for the date see n. 3.

⁶⁶Sharon, Vt., Land Records, vol. 5, p. 313 (Aug. 27, 1804). Solomon Mack is "of Tunbridge," according to the deed. This deed

recites $800 as consideration for the farm. However, a later deed recites a mortgage incurred on the date of purchase, in the amount of $441, showing that Solomon Mack paid $359 not raised by the mortgage. These terms are given in a possible second mortgage, in force about six weeks (vol. 6, p. 83, Mar. 21, 1807), which names "one mortgage deed against said land given by me to Daniel Gilbert . . . dated August 27, 1804, conditioned for the payment of $441 with annual interest in three years from the date, on which $14.27 by way of interest have been paid."

[67]See Lucy Smith, *Biographical Sketches*, p. 56, referring to Sharon, Vt.: "In the latter place my husband rented a farm of my father." Cp. the deed of May 3, 1806, wherein Daniel Mack (Solomon's son) conveys a lot in Tunbridge to Solomon Mack "of Sharon." Perhaps this is the place that Solomon moved to (even prior to this formal conveyance) while Joseph and Lucy Smith rented his farm. Tunbridge, Vt., Land Records, vol. 3, p. 380. It is doubtful that any residence is indicated by the double listing of Solomon Mack (Sr. and Jr.) on a Mar. 1803 voting list in the town records of Gilsum, N. H.

[68]Lucy Smith reports their move from Sharon back to Tunbridge, where Samuel Harrison Smith was born on Mar. 13, 1808.

[69]Sharon, Vt., Land Records, vol. 5, p. 83. This was a conveyance of the whole farm to Truman Miller, who some six weeks later and for the same consideration ($800) conveyed the property back to Solomon Mack "of Sharon." Sharon, Vt., Land Records, vol. 6, p. 99. This was perhaps a second mortgage; Solomon Mack had not moved, since the land is still referred to in Miller's reconveyance as "the farm that the said Solomon now lives on."

[70]See also the attempted deed of gift of the Solomon Mack farm to his son Jason's first child, made Mar. 20, 1810, in which Solomon refers to himself as "of Sharon." Sharon, Vt., Land Records, vol. 6, p. 386.

[71]Sharon, Vt., Land Records, vol. 6, p. 459. The deed conveys to Daniel Gilbert "one hundred acres, being the same farm I now live on and the same which I heretofore mortgaged to the said Gilbert." In 1811 Gilbert gave $500 for the land Solomon had bought for $800 in 1804 (n. 66). The same amount of $800 is named as the consideration in the deeds to and from Miller in 1806-07 (n. 69). Gilbert's lesser consideration in 1811 is probably explained by Gilbert's initial mortgage, mentioned in the above quotation from the

1811 conveyance and also the 1807 double deeds (n. 66). The $441 obligation of 1804 was evidently a purchase-money mortgage, paid down to around $300 by 1811. Solomon got $500 then, according to his deed, probably his clear equity in the place.

[72]Affidavit of Benjamin Cole Latham, Nov. 14, 1905, xerox of signed original in Vermont Property File, LDS Legal Department; also recorded Mar. 13, 1906, in the Sharon Town Record Book, a photocopy of which was furnished by Larry C. Porter. A somewhat imperfect copy is printed in *Proceedings at the Dedication of the Joseph Smith Memorial Monument* (n.p., n.d.), pp. 35-36. Latham's brief biography appears in Evelyn M. Wood Lovejoy, *History of Royalton, Vermont* (Burlington, Vt., 1911), p. 848. He is recalling the opinion of a contemporary of Solomon Mack, the Ebenezer Dewey whose dates are 1762-1833. See ibid., p. 760. Latham's affidavit also reports of Mack's residence from the same Ebenezer Dewey, whose farm adjoined Solomon Mack's: "I heard the elder Dewey say that Mack lived there in the house that then stood upon these foundations, both before and after Joseph Smith lived in it."

[73]Letter of Daniel Woodward, *Boston Transcript,* cit. *Historical Magazine,* vol. 8, 2d ser. (Nov. 1870), p. 316. Woodward's stories on Joseph Smith, Sr., are clearly garbled, but he was only seven when the Smiths moved to New Hampshire in 1811 and obviously had limited knowledge of adult transactions. Since he was born Apr. 15, 1804, he was in his teens when Solomon Mack moved from the Sharon-Royalton area, and he probably saw Solomon ride about; the omitted part of the quotation equates the sidesaddle with a "woman's saddle," perhaps just what critical adolescents were saying about Solomon. Woodward's biography is found in Lovejoy, *History of Royalton,* pp. 1041-42. Solomon refers to riding "sideways" because of injuries (*Narrative,* p. 12) and also mentions constant riding during Vermont years (*Narrative,* pp. 18, 25, 44).

[74]"Vermonter," unidentified but informed about the Sharon-Royalton neighborhood, commenting specifically on the prior reference to "Mr. Mack, of whom Judge Woodard speaks." There is no reason to question "Vermonter's" identification of himself: "I am a native of Royalton, Vermont, and resided in that town for a long period." *Boston Transcript,* cit. *Historical Magazine,* vol. 8, 2d ser. (Nov. 1870), p. 316.

[75]From immediate descendants, the 1881 town history reported of Solomon: "He removed to Tunbridge, Vt., and in his old age re-

turned to Gilsum and resided with his son." Hayward, *History of the Town of Gilsum*, p. 207; cp. n. 79.

⁷⁶Solomon Mack, Jr., is listed in 1819 with the same substantial property of other years, but "Solomon Mack" Sr.'s taxable property in 1819 is one horse. Only Solomon Mack, Jr., appears on the tax list of 1820. The son resided in Gilsum constantly and was referred to in the town records simply as Solomon Mack, but "Jr." is added in 1819 and 1820 to distinguish him from his father. Gilsum Town Records, State Copy, vol. 1, pp. 755-56. Cp. n. 54.

⁷⁷For a photograph and transcription of the gravestone, see Bennett, "Solomon Mack," vol. 59, pp. 90-91. The stone is identical with a transcription made in 1881 by Hayward, *History of the Town of Gilsum*, p. 64.

⁷⁸Mack, *Narrative*, p. 24.

⁷⁹Hayward, *History of the Town of Gilsum*, p. 207. An unusually specific town historian, Hayward probably got information in part from grandson Solomon Mack III, born the same year as Joseph Smith, Jr. (1805). When the town history was written in 1881, he was described as still retaining "the spirit and witty geniality of his youthful days" (p. 240).

⁸⁰Cp. n. 67 and the appearance of Joseph Smith, Sr., as a witness to Solomon Mack's deeds of Aug. 27, 1804, and May 3, 1806, the time that the Smiths rented Solomon Mack's farm. Sharon, Vt., Land Records, vol. 5, p. 313, and Tunbridge, Vt., Land Records, vol. 3, p. 380. Lucy Smith mentions that her mother "had lived with us some time" prior to 1816 (*Biographical Sketches*, p. 68). See also the earlier description of her mother's intense care for Lucy Smith during a critical illness about 1802 (pp. 46-47). Although her father was undoubtedly in the home from time to time, he may not appear in the narrative because of the more intimate relationship between mother and daughter.

⁸¹Lucy Mack Smith's *Biographical Sketches* (p. 18) quotes Solomon as identifying Lydia's father as "a man of wealth," the equivalent phrase of Lucy's preliminary manuscript being "a man living in ease and affluence." Solomon-Lucy both misname the father, Nathan Gates, also the name of a son; true identity is shown in the will of Daniel Gates, of East Haddam, which names one of his "loving daughters" as "Lydia Mack." Daniel Gates is also named as Lydia's father in the civil record of her marriage (n. 24) and in the

church record of her baptism (n. 82). He is called Deacon Daniel Gates in the record of proceedings probating his will (Probate Records, Colchester, Conn., vol. 4, pp. 154-56, 232, 293, 301), as also the Connecticut Vital Records Index of his death (Oct. 5, 1775) and that of his widow, Lydia Fuller Gates. There is probably documentary basis for the details of Daniel's life given in the genealogical sketch of his wife, who married "Daniel Gates, b. Feb. 5, 1706, a tanner of East Haddam (Millington). He was a deacon and selectman." William Hyslop Fuller, *Genealogy of Some Descendants of Edward Fuller of the Mayflower*, vol. 1 (Palmer, Mass., 1908), p. 43.

Deacon Daniel Gates is prominent in the church records of the First Congregational Church of East Haddam, Conn., and also the Second Congregational Church of East Haddam (Millington), where entries identify the baptisms of his children. Birth and baptism dates of his children are conveniently found in D. Williams Patterson, "George Gates of East Haddam, Connecticut, and His Descendants" (Long Island Historical Society ms., 1865), p. 21. Cp. ibid., p. 8, which also names Daniel Gates as a tanner, prominent in church affairs, and selectman of East Haddam in 1739.

The will of Lydia Gates' father contains a very detailed expression of faith, adding to the portion quoted the more ordinary phraseology of receiving his body back in the resurrection of the just. Probate Records, Colchester, Conn., vol. 4, pp. 154-56. His estate was able to meet all debts, bequests, and expenses, with the exception of 22 pounds, for which the assembly authorized his executor-son Nathan to sell a portion of real estate, Jan. 1778. Charles J. Hoadly (ed.), *Public Records of the State of Connecticut*, vol. 1 (Hartford, 1894), p. 492.

[82]According to the Fuller and Gates genealogies cited in n. 81, Lydia Gates Mack was born Sept. 3, 1732, in East Haddam. Her baptismal entry is found in the record of the First Congregational Church of East Haddam, vol. 1, p. 21: "Oct. 29, 1732, Br. Dan'l Gates's child was baptized and called Lydia." Although Lydia probably made an earlier profession of faith, her adult commitment is evidenced by the record of the Second Congregational Church of East Haddam (Millington), vol. 1, p. 19 (25), a list of individuals "received to communion": "July 25, 1762: Lydia Mack, wife of Solomon Mack." Perhaps this entry reflects a visit home for Lydia, possibly for the birth of a child.

[83]Lydia's illness is reported in Lucy Smith, *Biographical Sketches*, p. 36. The date is derived from Lucy's statement that she was then

eight. For Lydia Mack's influence on Solomon, see his *Narrative,* pp. 22-23.

[84]These two quotations on Lydia are from Solomon's fuller narrative, as quoted in Lucy Smith's preliminary manuscript (cp. n. 29). Her *Biographical Sketches,* p. 18, contains similar comments attributed to her father, Solomon.

[85]The indented quotation is from Solomon Mack's fuller journal, quoted by Lucy Smith, *Biographical Sketches,* p. 19. The remaining language is also attributed to Solomon Mack in Lucy's preliminary manuscript. Cp. n. 29.

[86]Lucy Smith describes Jason's early life in *Biographical Sketches,* pp. 21-23, later adding further material and quoting an 1835 letter from him, pp. 52-54. Cp. n. 46.

Lucy Smith's *Biographical Sketches* and her preliminary manuscript quote Solomon regarding Marlow, "where we remained until we had four children." These sources give 1761 for the move to Marlow, where Solomon appears in local records until 1773, by which time six children had been born. Since Solomon's marriage was Jan. 4, 1759 (n. 24), two children might have been born prior to the Marlow move in 1761; the "four children" might therefore mean that four children came in Marlow days, the four born 1762-70 (see below). Lucy's *Biographical Sketches* place fifth child Stephen's birth "in the town of Marlow June 15, 1766" (p. 30); she then places the birth of the two youngest children, Solomon and herself, in Gilsum, N. H. (pp. 35-36). Gilsum town records confirm her own birth there July 8, 1775 (n. 97).

In addition to the two definite birth dates named, two others may be approximated from their ages on gravestones at Gilsum, N.H.: Lydia Mack Bill died "Jan. 8, 1826, Ae. 62" (Hayward, *History of the Town of Gilsum,* p. 73); Solomon Mack, Jr., died "Oct. 12, 1851, Ae. 78" (ibid., p. 64), and the 1850 census of Gilsum gives 77 as his age the year before and confirms N.H. birth.

The births of the Mack children are as follows, with rough estimates indicated by *c.* (Latin *circa*): Jason, c. 1760; Lovisa, c. 1761; Lovina, c. 1762; Lydia, 1764; Stephen, June 15, 1766; Daniel, c. 1770; Solomon, 1773; Lucy, July 8, 1775.

[87]The dramatic deaths of Lovisa and Lovina remarkably parallel each other, but Lovina's story is not detailed in chapter 4 because it is not detailed in Solomon Mack's writings. Her dying testimony of

God to her family and friends is given in Lucy Smith, *Biographical Sketches,* pp. 26-28.

[88]Lucy's preliminary manuscript surveys his Tunbridge operations: "he built here a store, a very large tavern, and cultivated an extensive farm." Cp. *Biographical Sketches,* pp. 30-33. In less than ten years at Tunbridge, he and his partner John Mudget have two dozen real estate transactions indexed, and Stephen Mack has another dozen by himself. His purchase of a pew in the town meetinghouse Sept. 2, 1801, is also recorded. Tunbridge, Vt., Land Records, vol. 5, p. 198.

Stephen Mack's remarkable life is summarized well in two sources: Lillian Drake Avery, "Revolutionary Soldiers of Oakland County," *Michigan Historical Collections,* vol. 39 (1915), pp. 438-40; Bennett, "Solomon Mack," vol. 59, pp. 154-55, 190-91, 246.

His obituary appeared in the *Detroit Gazette,* Nov. 14, 1826, the complete text of which is: "Col. Stephen Mack, a soldier of the Revolution, an enterprising and industrious citizen, and a kind and provident father, departed this life last Saturday morning at Pontiac, in the seventy-second year of his age. Col. M. has for nearly twenty years resided in this territory, and has been distinguished from the mass of his fellow-citizens for his enterprise and the great utility of his views. It is owing to his exertions more than to any other man's, that the first settlers of Oakland County were so soon accomodated with mills and other useful works. His sacrifices and his exertions in promoting the best interests of the new county, which he had been so eminently useful in settling and organizing, endeared him to his fellow-citizens, and confiding in his excellent judgment in all matters connected with the welfare of a young community, they elected him to the first legislative council of the territory. His advanced age constantly warned him that he had but a short time to remain with us; yet he stayed not his labors, and death found him striving to accomplish objects of the most useful and permanent kind. The loss of such a man is truly that of the public—and many are those who share the grief of the numerous family which he has left."

[89]Letter of Hyrum Smith to "Mrs. Hariet M. Whittemer," Apr. 9, 1843, Nauvoo, Ill., Univ. of Mich. ms. Hariett Whittemore was Stephen Mack's daughter and Hyrum Smith's cousin. Hayward, *History of the Town of Gilsum,* supplies information on the local prominence of Solomon Mack, Jr., and includes his gravestone inscription: "SOLOMON MACK, Died Oct. 12, 1851, Ae. 78. Tread

softly by this sacred spot, / Where parents sleep, though not forgot. / In life we shared their love; / May we in heaven meet them above" (p. 64).

⁹⁰Ibid., p. 73. Cp. n. 56.

⁹¹Joseph Smith, Manuscript History, Note A; at the beginning of the trip "we were accompanied by my mother's mother."

⁹²Lucy Smith, *Biographical Sketches,* p. 68. Lucy's preliminary manuscript corrects the impression that Lydia Gates Mack lived permanently with the Joseph Smith family, or intended to accompany them to New York: "My mother was with me. She had been assisting in my preparations for traveling. She was now returning to her home."

⁹³Joseph Smith, Manuscript History, Note A. He remembered his grandmother's being injured by a capsizing sleigh; Lucy Smith's memory of the injury from a wagon is preferred on the ground that she would more vividly remember circumstances associated with her mother. Lydia Mack remained at Royalton, where she stayed with her son Daniel Mack until death, "which was two years afterwards." Lucy Smith, *Biographical Sketches,* pp. 68-69. Since the New York move was probably 1816, the death of Lydia Gates Mack was about 1818.

Lucy's preliminary manuscript makes clear that Lydia Gates Mack was "now returning to her home." Apparently Solomon and his wife lived with their son Daniel at Royalton at certain times after selling their Sharon farm in 1811.

⁹⁴Lucy Smith, *Biographical Sketches,* pp. 68-69, reports the parting scene and close of Lydia Mack's life. The last charge of Lydia is very similar in *Biographical Sketches* and the preliminary manuscript, though the spontaneous quality of the latter is significant and has been quoted, including Lucy Smith's longer appraisal of her mother found there.

⁹⁵See "Circumstantial Confirmation of the First Vision Through Reminiscences," *Brigham Young University Studies,* vol. 9 (Spring 1969), pp. 390-91.

⁹⁶"Map of Montague, Surveyed in [1794] by Elisha Root," published in Edward Pearson Pressey, *History of Montague* (Montague, Mass., 1910), facing p. 80. Although at this location "1764" is given as the date of the map, it is elsewhere described as made in 1794.

In Robert P. Clapp's 1895 address in this history, the map is described with background historical information (p. 29): "I have here a tracing of a map of the town, made by Elisha Root in 1794, showing the main roads, the ferries, mills and taverns. . . . Four taverns appear . . . Severance's, on the east of Federal Street, a little south of Dry Hill Road, and Taft's (afterwards Durkee's), nearly a mile south of the mouth of Miller's River on the Northfield Road. Was Martin Root's tavern, then, in 1794, abandoned? It is not shown on the map. The old sign, dated 1785, now in the Memorial Hall at Deerfield, used to swing from the original Joseph Root house. . . . Martin was but thirty-two years old in 1785 and died in 1833." Clapp clearly understood the map as made in 1794, and the 1785 tavern sign supports that date. See also Pressey's reference to "a map of 1794, surveyed by Elisha Root" (ibid., p. 138). Other references to the Severance and Taft taverns are ibid., pp. 135-36, 141. The corresponding names on the 1790 Montague census are Moses Severance and Lyman Taft, the latter a proprietor with Elisha Mack for the Connecticut River toll bridge. Cp. n. 53.

[97]Lucy gives her birthdate as July 8, 1776, in *Biographical Sketches* (p. 36). However, the Gilsum, N. H., town record is presumably accurate in recording her birth a year earlier: July 8, 1775. For Lovisa's marriage, see n. 102.

[98]*Vital Records of Montague,* p. 135 (Montague Deaths): "Gunn, Asahel, Capt., July 11, 1796, in his 65th y," citing "gravestone record, Old South Cemetery, Montague." The DAR record of this cemetery differs slightly in wording but agrees on dates and the title of "Capt. Asahel Gunn." Montague, Franklin County, Mass., Cemetery Records (n.p., n.d.), p. 20.

[99]Sylvester Judd, *History of Hadley* (Northampton, Mass., 1863), p. 406, footnote; cp. p. 402. For items on Woodbridge's prominence, see pp. 393-94, 397 (footnote), 412, 603.

An early family history gives the dates of his life (Mar. 5, 1739, to Mar. 8, 1819) and the following understanding of his career: "He never married; he was a col. in the army of the Revolution. . . . Was a man of large wealth (for those days) and of great influence in the town of South Hadley, Mass., where he always resided." Rev. John Woodbridge, *The Woodbridge Record* (New Haven, Conn., 1883), n. 54 therein.

[100]See Clifton Johnson, *Historic Hampshire in the Connecticut Valley* (Springfield, Mass., 1932), pp. 162-63: "Soon after the Revolu-

tion Colonel Ruggles Woodbridge, the richest man in town, built his beautiful home, now known as the Hollingsworth house. He was an original thinker, and when he opened in his mansion the 'Woodbridge School for Boys,' it was an immediate success. He was compelled to add wing after wing to his house until people said that if it had a few more, it would be able to fly. On Sundays the pupils were obliged to dress in uniform and march two and two into the meetinghouse with military precision. Most of them came from old and aristocratic families, and they wore tall hats. Those hats gave great offense to the town boys, and between them and the wearers of the hats there were numerous collisions in which fists were freely used. A considerable list might be given of governors and other leading men who were educated at the school."

[101]I am indebted to Anne E. Savacheck, Town Clerk of South Hadley, Mass., for an attested copy of minutes pertaining to the bell in the Town Record Book entitled "Meetings—District, 1753-1775; Town, 1775-1825; Miscellaneous, 1730-1847." Relevant extracts from this copy (May 21, 1971) follow, entered by date from the Town of South Hadley minutes of meetings:

May 2, 1791: "Voted that the selectmen return the thanks of the town to Col. R. Woodbridge for his liberal offer to them respecting his giving a bell to the town."

May 16, 1791: "Voted that the town will build a belfry and steeple." A committee was appointed and money appropriated "to the use of building a steeple."

Jan 12, 1792: "Voted to raise 65 pounds to be expended in building a belfry and steeple." Two were added to the building committee, one of which was "Col. R. Woodbridge."

June 18, 1792: "It was tried by a vote whether the town will move the north gallery stairs into the steeple—passed in the negative. . . . Voted that committee for building the belfry be a committee for shingling the meeting house."

Nov. 8, 1792: "Voted to raise the sum of 280 pounds to defray the expense of building the belfry and repairing the meeting house."

Sept. 1793: "Upon a report of the belfry committee that Mr. Amos Doolittle . . . proposed to recast the town's meeting house bell a second time for the sum of 15 pounds . . . and further, should the bell fail or not be good after a second recasting, he would take it at the meeting house in South Hadley and return a good bell to the same place free from any cost of transporation to the town. Voted that Col. R. Woodbridge, Ens. J. A. Smith and

David Smith be a committee to employ Mr. Doolittle to recast the bell a second time."

[102]*Vital Records of Montague, Massachusetts* (Salem, Mass., 1934), pp. 91, 118. The marriage is indexed under groom Joseph Tuttle and bride Lovisa Mack, both locations giving Jan. 31, 1780, as the date, and both annotated "intention not recorded." Mr. Bernard McCarthy, present Montague town clerk, courteously confirms this date as correctly copied from the town records, and adds that Moses Gunn performed the marriage (letter of May 1971).

[103]Basic surveys of known dates and census information are available on Lovisa's father-in-law, John (1726-1795?); her husband, Joseph (1756-1816); and his son Joseph (1796-1884) in Alva M. Tuttle, *Tuttle-Tuthill Lines in America* (Columbus, Ohio, 1968), pp. 311, 338, 340. For biographical information on the author, Joseph Tuttle, see the *Biographical History* entry cited in n. 50, and his *Painesville Telegraph* obituary Ap. 24, 1884, indicating his residence at Concord, Ohio, for 67 years and characterizing him as "a man of energy and enterprise, well known and esteemed throughout this section of the country."

[104]"Narrative of the Life of Joseph Tuttle," location and origin discussed in n. 50 above. One would assume a family Bible entry or some definite tradition to name Lovisa's death "fourteen years after marriage." This would logically have been fixed in the mind of young Joseph Tuttle because of his birthdate, given in his "Narrative" as May 10, 1796, and the preceding remarriage of his father about 1795, at which time Lovisa was dead. The point of Lovisa's childlessness is reinforced at the beginning of the younger Joseph's "Narrative": "I was the oldest of my father's nine children." Although Tuttle considered that Solomon Mack lived in the same town as his father and grandfather, Sunderland, all evidence indicates that Mack resided in the adjoining Montague.

[105]Lucy Smith's preliminary manuscript gives the information that Lovisa was the "oldest" and Lovina the "youngest," meaning younger, since Lydia was younger than Lovisa. Cp. *Biographical Sketches*, p. 21: "The history of Lovisa and Lovina, my two oldest sisters." Comparison of the chronological chart and the accounts of Lucy Smith printed in this chapter give data on the deaths of Lovisa and Lovina. Near the end of the preliminary discussion of this chapter is another quotation from Lucy Smith's preliminary manuscript that speaks of Lovisa as "my oldest sister" and Lovina as "her sister next to her."

[106]At sister Lovina's death, shortly before Lovisa's, Lucy carried her "in my arms . . . although I was but thirteen years old." *Biographical Sketches,* p. 27. Based on her understanding of a 1776 birthdate (cp. n. 97), Lovisa's death might be estimated as 1789. However, there is room for error in recollection, since Lovina had a protracted illness, and Lucy might remember carrying her emaciated body long before her death about 1794. There is only one other chronological statement in Lucy Smith that seems confused for this early period. In the preliminary manuscript she says that Lovina "was taken with the consumption at 16 and languished 3 years with this fatal disease." One might read the statement to mean that Lovina died at age 19 (about 1781), but Lucy may have meant that Lovisa was chronically ill from 16 and critically ill the last three years of her life. This hint of such an extended sickness sheds light on Lucy's memory of carrying Lovisa when Lucy herself was only 13 years of age.

[107]Lucy Mack Smith's comments on her marriage show that she considered the deaths of her sisters not much earlier than that, an event dated by the Tunbridge, Vt., town records in 1796, a date which she also furnishes. In fact, her narrative gives one further method for dating her sisters' deaths. Describing Lovisa's funeral in her preliminary manuscript, Lucy closes with this sentence: "I was then in Tunbridge with brother S[tephen] Mack." Census and town records firmly locate Stephen Mack in Gilsum, New Hampshire, from 1789 to 1793, from which time he is found at Tunbridge, Vt.; so the earliest known time for residing with Stephen in Tunbridge is 1793. See, for instance, Stephen Mack's conveyances Aug. 24, 1793, and Aug. 20, 1794, at Tunbridge, Vt., in both of which he names his residence "of Tunbridge." Tunbridge, Vt., Land Records, vol. 1, p. 467; vol. 2, p. 59. Incidentally, this fits Lucy's maximum time of about two years from Lovisa's death (when Lucy was at Tunbridge) until Lucy's marriage Jan. 24, 1796.

[108]Solomon Mack's family's profile on the 1790 census implies that Lovina was still alive. Although Solomon had four boys and four girls, Jason and Stephen had left home by then, and the accompanying chronology chart shows that two girls were already married. That year at Montague, Mass., three males and three females were counted, no doubt the parents and two boys and two girls, one of the latter probably Lovina Mack. For a list of children, see n. 86. Cp. chronological chart, pp. 68-69.

[109]Lucy Smith mentions the last communication home from Lovisa: "[M]y father received a letter from South Hadley, stating that Lovisa was very low of the consumption." *Biographical Sketches,* p. 26. The preliminary manuscript mentions the visit to Lovisa, "then sick at South Hadley," which took place "two years before sister Lovina's death." The quotation is found in full near the beginning of this chapter.

[110]Lucy Smith remembers that Lovina went to Lovisa's "and remained with her sister during her illness, which lasted two years" (*Biographical Sketches,* p. 23). This was before Lovisa's healing, estimated as about 1791 (chronological chart, pp. 68-69). One would therefore suspect that Lovina is the additional female in the Joseph Tuttle household in 1790 (cp. n. 104), though Lovina also appears to be enumerated in the Solomon Mack household (n. 108). The same person could be counted in two locations because of differing local days of enumeration. Lovina might also have been counted personally with the Tuttles, and also recorded in her father's household as a resident, though temporarily away.

[111]John Tuttle is enumerated in Sunderland, Mass., in 1790, with 1 male over 16, 1 male under 16, and 3 females. Yet John Tuttle, Sr. (1726-1795?), and John Tuttle, Jr. (1763-1829), both lived in Sunderland in this period. Joseph Tuttle's "Narrative" indicates that the younger John Tuttle had children by his first wife, who died; he remarried July 20, 1790. John Montague Smith, *History of the Town of Sunderland* (Greenfield, Mass., 1899), p. 560, gives this definite date, and Town Clerk Ellen M. Korpita has courteously verified it in the Sunderland town records. Since the census began the first Monday in August (that year Aug. 4), perhaps the newly married couple was away, but the children of John's prior marriage were enumerated in the household of John Tuttle, Sr. Family tradition was that both Tuttles lived in Sunderland near each other. Cp. the enlistment of young John Tuttle in 1779, "age, 16 yrs . . . engaged for town of Sunderland." *Massachusetts Soldiers and Sailors of the Revolutionary War,* vol. 16 (Boston, 1907), p. 206. At Sunderland, July 14, 1792, one John Tuttle signed a petition for exemption from Congregational Church assessments because of Baptist belief, a document copied from the town archives by the helpfulness of Mrs. W. L. Hubbard.

[112]"Narrative of the Life of Joseph Tuttle." No probate court record of John Tuttle's death is available in the Massachusetts records. However, only the younger John Tuttle family appears on the

1800 census, by which time John Tuttle, Sr., had evidently died. Birthdates of the younger John Tuttle's children correspond to his family on the 1800 census. Tuttle, *Tuttle-Tuthill Lines* (cit. n. 103), p. 312, gives these birthdates, based on Harley Angelo Tuttle, *The Palmyra Tuttles* (Palmyra, Ohio, 1922), p. 6, and Smith, *History of the Town of Sunderland* (cit. n. 111), p. 560. Inquiries have produced a single deed, a conveyance on Feb. 16, 1780, of about 20 acres to John Tuttle of Sunderland. Franklin County, Mass., Land Records, Hampshire Abstracts, vol. 3, p. 264.

[113]The accounts are edited upon the principles outlined at the beginning of chapter 3. Brackets enclose my additions, with one substitution: "ate" for the printed reading "eat." Lucy's preliminary manuscript is included for its richness of personal detail, sometimes simplified in the final draft. The preliminary manuscript is occasionally disjointed, necessitating the arrangement of isolated sentences in sequence. I have deleted words if they represent a first writing that was deleted.

[114]Isaac Watts, *Psalms of David, Imitated,* 116th Psalm, first part. Solomon Mack's *Narrative* identifies the hymn sung by Lovisa. The stanza following from the same psalm is hereafter quoted. No edition is cited here for Watts, since several have been checked in the years of publication likely used, and the stanzas quoted are the same in each. The solid popularity of Watts' *Psalms* in eighteenth-century America is attested by their constant reprinting. Cp. an informed opinion on this subject: "By the early years of the nineteenth century the more conservative elements in the New England churches had come to regard Watts with almost the same veneration which their forefathers a hundred years earlier had accorded to *The Bay Psalm Book.*" Henry Wilder Foote, *Three Centuries of American Hymnody* (Hamden, Conn., 1961), p. 165.

[115]For New England genealogy before Samuel, see Mary Audentia Smith Anderson, *Ancestry and Posterity of Joseph Smith and Emma Hale* (Independence, Mo., 1929), particularly his father's Smith line (pp. 51-59) and his mother's Gould line (pp. 99-105). Priscilla Gould bore a name synonymous with public service and courageous dissent. Her father was a militia lieutenant and once selectman at Topsfield. Her grandfather John Gould was repeatedly selectman and state legislator; "few names are more frequently found in the town, county, and court records." George Francis Dow, *History of Topsfield, Massachusetts* (Topsfield, 1940), p. 26.

Descendants were proud of his imprisonment and punishment for sedition in speaking against harsh Colonial government; also proverbial was the individualism of his father, the original Zaccheus Gould, one of Topsfield's founders. For civil offices held, see D. Hamilton Hurd, *History of Essex County, Massachusetts* (Philadelphia, 1888), vol. 2, pp. 984-86. Cp. n. 157, and Benjamin Apthorp Gould, *The Family of Zaccheus Gould of Topsfield* (Lynn, Mass., 1895), pp. 25-46.

[116]Hurd, *History of Essex County* (cit. n. 115), vol. 2, pp. 984-87.

[117]For detailed lists of public service, see Joseph F. Smith, Jr. (President Joseph Fielding Smith), "Asahel Smith of Topsfield, with Some Account of the Smith Family," *Historical Collections of the Topsfield Historical Society,* vol. 8 (1902), pp. 88-89; and Anderson, *Ancestry and Posterity of Joseph Smith,* pp. 55-59.

[118]For instance, see Samuel's election as one of the three constituting the Topsfield Committee for Correspondence, May 18, 1773. *Town Records of Topsfield, Massachusetts,* vol. 2 (Topsfield, 1920), pp. 318-20. He was also elected to the Tea Committee at Topsfield on Jan. 6, 1774, which led out in agreeing with the Boston opposition and sympathizing with Boston's destruction of tea the previous month. Ibid., pp. 323-24. See also Samuel Smith's 1774 elections to the Ipswich Convention and the First Provincial Congress. Dow, *History of Topsfield,* p. 169.

[119]Will of Samuel Smith, Mar. 3, 1767, Essex County Registry of Probate, File 25750. Incidentally, Samuel Smith, Samuel's father, also was religiously committed, judged by his statement of faith in "my merciful creator and redeemer" in the preamble of his own will, Mar. 26, 1748. Essex County Registry of Probate, File 25744.

Samuel Smith of Rowley was involved in a brawl in 1685, but the date of marriage, family married into, and residence do not fit Asael Smith's grandfather. At least one writer has jumped to a false conclusion in reading Dow, *History of Topsfield,* pp. 128, 372. This Samuel Smith of Rowley is identified (and his correct in-laws) in George B. Blodgette, "Early Settlers of Rowley, Mass.," *Essex Institute Historical Collections,* vol. 22 (1885), p. 306, and vol. 20 (1883), pp. 78-79.

[120]See church entry of Jan. 2, 1737: "Samuel Smith, Jr. and Priscilla his wife owned the covenant." "Records of the Congregational Church in Topsfield," *Historical Collections of . . . Topsfield,*

vol. 14 (1909), p. 32. For dates of baptism of Samuel's five children, see George Francis Dow, "Baptismal Records of the Church in Topsfield," *Historical Collections of . . . Topsfield,* vol. 1 (1895), pp. 9, 10, 11, 13, and 15, the last entry noting Asael, son of Samuel Smith, as baptized Mar. 11, 1744.

Samuel's prestige in the closing years of his life is evident in his appointment to important church committees of discipline and representation in 1783-84. George Francis Dow, "Records of the Congregational Church in Topsfield," *Historical Collections of . . . Topsfield,* vol. 14 (1909), pp. 70, 74, 76-77, 79. Samuel was prominent in the status-oriented assignment of pews, appearing in the first grouping after the elders (the "men's first seat below") on a list probably made in 1771, when his son Samuel appears in the "men's first seat in the front gallery." In this year the town appointed "Capt. Samuel Smith" to a committee "to seat the inhabitants of the town in the meeting house." Presumably it is the father and not the son Samuel who appears in the "first seat in the front gallery" in a similar list of 1762. "The Seating in the Meeting House, 1762 and 1771," *Historical Collections of . . . Topsfield,* vol. 7 (1901), pp. 93, 98-100; also cit. Dow, *History of Topsfield,* pp. 255, 259, 60.

Cp. Samuel's direction for his wife in his will: "And I also order my said sons to provide her a horse to ride to meeting whenever she shall have occasion during the time she shall remain my widow."

[121]*Salem* [Mass.] *Gazette,* Nov. 22, 1785. Asael early displayed responsible traits of his father Samuel. Writing to George A. Smith in 1870 about Asael Smith, Humphrey Gould recalled seeing a letter that Asael had written as a "grown-up young man" to his uncle, challenging disparaging reports about the daughters of his grandfather: "He began his letter thus, 'Venerable Uncle,' and then went on to make a statement of his complaint. . . . This letter I have read several times, and it is still extant or was the last I knew. He could not endure the thought of having the six daughters scandalized. I dare say they were girls full of life and animation, and nothing strange if somebody was jealous of them. What pleased me was the veneration with which he approached his uncle and the sensitive nature of your grandfather." Gould to Smith, May 26, 1870, Rowe, Mass.

[122]Asael Smith's birthdate is given in his own hand in the family Bible: "I Asael Smith was born March the 7th, 1744." The town

record entry gives "Asael, s. Samuel and Priscilla, Mar. 7, 1743-4." This second record also means 1744, inasmuch as the first three months of the year prior to 1752 might be written in the double system of the new year beginning in January or early spring. *Vital Records of Topsfield, Massachusetts to the End of the Year 1849* (Topsfield, Mass., 1903), pp. 3, 94. Although a few early records of his life have "Asahel" Smith, I have followed the predominant "Asael," the spelling of his own signature in the Bible and the documents reproduced in chapter 6.

[123]Essex County Land Records, vol. 113, p. 144 (Mar. 24, 1763); vol. 145, p. 109 (Apr. 10, 1764). The first farm is described in the deed as "lying partly in Topsfield and partly in Boxford," and the second deed conveys "a certain messuage and dwelling house and barn with about seventy-five acres of land, be it more or less, in Topsfield . . . beginning at Pye Brook. . . ." The earliest known reference to this house is by Alfred P. Putnam, "Danvers, at Home and Abroad, No. 58," Aug. 22, 1885, *Danvers* [Mass.] *Mirror,* Aug. 29, 1885: "[H]ere was the home of the immediate ancestors of 'Joe Smith,' the Mormon prophet. I have visited the spot, a mile or two north of the village, where they lived. The old house which they once occupied was torn down nine or ten years ago. . . . No doubt there is a certain quiet spot beside a gentle stream in the old town of Topsfield, which is yet to attract to itself many a Mormon Pilgrim." For background on Putnam, cp. n. 156.

[124]The Topsfield tax records are largely intact for this period. The land, crops, and animals are fairly constant on all assessment returns, showing a stable operation of the land over many years. The Pye Brook location is part of the metes and bounds descriptions of the Smith deeds pertaining to this farm.

Detailed tax inventories are preserved fairly constantly from 1777 on, and the usual products mentioned are hay, corn, rye, barley, oats, beans, potatoes, turnips, and cider. Livestock is detailed from 1768 on, when Samuel, Sr., listed 2 horses, 2 oxen, 5 cows, 2 swine—and Samuel, Jr., listed 3 cows and 1 swine. In later years there were generally more animals, including a dozen or more sheep.

[125]Assessment lists of Topsfield are almost complete through these years. Asael appears first in 1765 with his father and brother. He appears also in 1768, though from 1769 on he is absent. Samuel Smith "and his son Samuel" continue to be assessed as property holders on the farm.

[126]Both family and town records agree on the date of marriage, Feb. 12, 1767. The family Bible (in possession of descendant David H. Horne, Salt Lake City, Utah) contains Asael's own notation: "Asael Smith was married to Mary Duty Feb. 12, 1767." Cp. *Vital Records of Topsfield,* p. 186: "Asael Smith and Mary Duty, of Wenham [Windham], N. H., Feb. 12, 1767." The same date was entered by Asael at the beginning of the first town record of Derry-field, N. H., when he was town clerk there. Cp. n. 140.

The year after his marriage, 1768, Asael appears on the poll tax list with his father and brother, though he is assigned no taxable property.

[127]Christenings of the children of Moses Duty are found in George B. Blodgette, "Early Records of Rowley, Massachusetts," *Essex Institute Historical Collections,* vol. 35 (1899), pp. 280 ff., with Asael's wife appearing on p. 281 as "Elisabeth Duty, daughter of Moses," christened Oct. 16, 1743. Her birth is recorded in town records as "Mary, d. Moses and Mary, Oct. 11, 1743," and the family later gave the name Elisabeth to a younger sister, noted also in town records: "Elizebeth (Deuty), d. Moses and Mary, Oct. 26, 1751." *Vital Records of Rowley, Massachusetts to the End of the Year 1849* (Salem, 1928), p. 72. Moses Duty's will names all of his children, including Elizabeth and "Mary Smith," whose husband Asael is named in the record of distribution. Probate Records, Rockingham County, Exeter, N. H., will proved Apr. 29, 1778. Its preamble contains a common expression of faith in God's power to raise his body at the general resurrection.

For Mary Duty Smith's family group, see George B. Blodgette, *Early Settlers of Rowley, Massachusetts* (Rowley, 1933), pp. 110-11, which notes that Mary appears as Elizabeth on the church record.

[128]*Vital Records of Topsfield,* pp. 95-96. Births are also recorded in Topsfield for Jesse (Apr. 20, 1768) and Priscilla (Oct. 21, 1769).

[129]George Francis Dow, "Baptismal Records of the Church in Topsfield," *Historical Collections of . . . Topsfield,* vol. 1 (1895), pp. 37-38: "Asael Smith, his Jesse, Mar. 8, 1772; Asael Smith, his Priscilla, Mar. 8, 1772; Asael Smith, his Joseph, Mar. 8, 1772."

Acceptance of the covenant appears in "Records of the Congregational Church" (cit. n. 120), p. 58. The actual form of Samuel and Asael's professions of faith are not preserved, but would have differed little from "the covenant of this church" adopted at Topsfield May 12, 1792, expressing acceptance of the Trinity, holy scripture, Christ's atonement, together with an obligation to live a Christian life and be subject to church government. Ibid., p. 86.

[130]Because of Asael's Topsfield roots, two more births were recorded there with the notation, "born Windham, N. H." These are for Asael, Jr. (May 21, 1773), and Mary (June 4, 1775). *Vital Records of Topsfield,* pp. 94, 96. The marriage record also notes that Mary Duty is "of Wenham [Windham], N. H." Ibid., p. 186.

[131]The pamphlet, discussed later in this chapter, is not presently locatable but was in possession of George A. Smith in 1870, when he described it in two letters and quoted portions of Asael's writings in it. Prefacing the quotation in the text is: "The following is written in Asael's own hand on a fly-leaf of the anti-slavery pamphlet referred to in a former letter, entitled 'A Caution to Great Britain and Her Colonies.' " Letter of George A. Smith to Humphrey Gould, June 10, 1870, Salt Lake City, Utah.

[132]Journal of Joseph Smith, July 9, 1843; the remark mentioned specifically "civil and religious liberty" and is quoted as the epigraph of this book, p. xix. Cp. n. 2.

[133]"A Roll of a Company Raised for Canada Service from Col. Thornton's and Col. Bartlet's Regiments," ms. at U. S. General Services Administration. The four officers appearing at the top of Asael Smith's muster roll headed Company 4 of Colonel Joshua Wingate's regiment, according to detailed history compiled from war records; the service of this unit is briefly noted: "The regiments under Cols. Wyman and Wingate were raised for the army of Canada, but joined the Northern Army in New York, Gen. Sullivan having made his successful retreat with the remnant of Montgomery's Army before their arrival." C. E. Potter, *Military History of the State of New Hampshire* (Concord, 1866), pp. 289-90. Asael Smith's company was recruited from Londonderry and nearby towns in southern New Hampshire. Edward L. Parker, *History of Londonderry* (Boston, 1851), pp. 337-38, verified by the printed rolls indicating Asael's service in July and Aug. 1776, in the "Londonderry or Nesmith Company." *Rolls of the Soldiers in the Revolutionary War, 1775 to May, 1777,* State Papers Series, vol. 14 (Concord, N. H., 1885), p. 342; cp. the reprint of the roll cited above, pp. 347-49.

In early Revolutionary years Asael Smith probably lived in nearby Salem, N. H., where an individual of that name appears in town records in 1776 and 1777. He signed the American loyalty oath there. *Miscellaneous Revolutionary Documents of New Hampshire,* State Papers Series, vol. 30 (Manchester, N. H., 1910), p. 134.

[134]John Smith, Journal, July 20, 1839. Cp. the summary of the human cost of fortifying the northern frontier in the fall and winter of Asael's service: "Like the story of Valley Forge, it is not told in startling deeds of blood. Though but few had perished by the sword, yet five thousand who had gone out at the call of their country never returned. More than one out of every three became the victims of pestilence, want, and exposure; and many of those who passed through the campaign came out of it with broken constitutions to fill premature graves." Charles Henry Jones, *History of the Campaign for the Conquest of Canada in 1776* (Philadelphia, 1882), p. 198.

[135]Asael Smith, Address to His Family, reproduced in chapter 6.

[136]See Hillsborough County, N. H., Land Records, vol. 14, p. 394 (May 27, 1778); Rockingham County, N. H., Land Records, vol. 121, p. 450 (Feb. 14, 1779); Hillsborough County, N. H., Land Records, vol. 19, p. 57 (Mar. 24, 1786); Essex County, Mass., Land Records, vol. 145, p. 192 (Mar. 24, 1786); vol. 148, p. 123 (May 30, 1787); vol. 152, p. 224 (Mar. 15, 1791). The writings of both William Smith and Lucy Mack Smith indicate the combination of coopering and farming occupations continued by Asael's second son, Joseph Smith, Sr.

[137]The quotation refers to Silas' northern New York occupation prior to his migration to Kirtland, Ohio, in 1836. *Genealogical and Family History of Northern New York* (New York, 1919), vol. 3, p. 930. Two sons of Silas returned to St. Lawrence County, New York, and descendants were probably consulted in compiling the detailed genealogies of this book. An incomplete manuscript of the early Utah period describes Asael as continuing the cooper's trade in Vermont, indicating that his son "Silas married Ruth Stevens with the understanding that they were to live together with his father in the cooper's shop." "Biography of John Smith, Patriarch," LDS Historian's Office. The document is dated 1854, the year of John Smith's death, and seems to be a collection of family traditions, all of which may not be firsthand.

[138]Hillsborough County, N. H., Land Records, vol. 14, p. 394. In this 1778 deed and the 1779 deed mentioned (n. 136), Asael's residence is recited as Derryfield, N. H. George A. Smith copied a Derryfield notation in Asael Smith's handwriting but in "different ink" from the Dunbarton notation in his anti-slavery pamphlet (cit. n. 131): "Derryfield, Sept. the 28, 1780."

[139]See the multiple references, pp. 290-375, *Early Records of the Town of Derryfield, Now Manchester, N. H., 1751-1782,* vol. 1, *Manchester Historic Association Collections,* vol. 8 (1905). See also the multiple references, pp. 12-100, *Early Records of the Town of Derryfield, Now Manchester, N. H., 1782-1800, Manchester Historic Association Collections,* vol. 9 (1906). Although Asael was again elected town clerk in Mar. 1786, and served in Apr., in May he was voted a settlement and a replacement was elected "for the curnt year." Ibid., 97-100.

[140]The following entries appear on the beginning pages of the first town record of Derryfield [Manchester] in Asael Smith's handwriting.

"February the 12th, 1767; then Asael Smith, the son of Capt. Samuel Smith and Priscilla Smith his wife was married to Mary, the daughter of Moses and Mary Duty. [Cp. n. 126.]

"April the 20th, 1768; then first son Jesse Smith was born, and October the 21st Priscilla, their daughter, was born, 1769.

"Joseph Smith, their third child, was born July the 12th, 1771, and May the twenty-first their fourth child, Asael Smith, was born, 1773.

"Mary Smith, their fifth child, was born June 4th, 1775.

"Samuel Smith, the sixth child of Asael and Mary Smith, was born September the 15th, 1777.

"The first five children above are recorded in Topsfield Records. [Cp. n. 128 and n. 129.]

"Recorded this sixth day of September, 1779, pr me, Asael Smith, Town [Clerk]."

"October the first, 1779; then Silas Smith, the son of Asael and Mary Smith, was born.

"Recorded October the first, 1779, pr me, Asael Smith, Town [Clerk]."

"May the 18th, 1783; Susannah Smith, the daughter of Asael Smith and Mary his wife, was born.

"Recorded this first day of June, 1783, pr me, Asael Smith, T. Clerk."

[141]John Smith, Journal, July 20, 1839, reproduced in chapter 7.

[142]Ibid., Samuel's death is noted as Nov. 14, 1785, and the cause named "apoplexy." *Vital Records of Topsfield,* p. 250. For the validity of the quotation marks editorially imposed, cp. n. 239.

[143]John Smith, Journal, July 20, 1839.

[144]John Smith wrote: "my father's own mother died at the time of his birth, and [he] was brought [up] by his stepmother (ibid.). The *Vital Records of Topsfield* confirm the basic accuracy of this report. Priscilla, wife of Samuel Smith, Jr., died Sept. 25, 1744 (p. 249), and her son Asael's birthdate was Mar. 7, 1744 (n. 122). Samuel next married his deceased wife's full cousin of the same name Oct. 8, 1745 (p. 187). This Priscilla Gould was born April 6, 1714 (p. 51), and died May 27, 1797 (p. 249). See Gould, *Family of Zaccheus Gould,* pp. 53-54, 64.

[145]John Smith, Journal, July 20, 1839. See also Asael's word to his wife in his family address (reproduced in chapter 6): "if you should marry again[,] remember what I have undergone by a stepmother, and do not estrange your husband from his own children or kindred, lest you draw on him and on yourself a great sin."

[146]Ibid., Although John Smith was nearing five when the move took place, he is undoubtedly reporting family information, and his factual structure is accurate. See, e.g., n. 147 and n. 148

[147]Hillsborough County, N. H., Land Records, vol. 19, pp. 47-48, deed of Asael Smith "of Derryfield . . . cooper," to Samuel Smith "of Topsfield . . . gentleman," Mar. 24, 1786, Mary Smith joining in the conveyance. The farm is the same deeded to Asael on May 27, 1778, though Asael's purchase of the approximately 100-acre farm was for 180 pounds, and his sale of the same land was for 120 pounds. He preserved the restriction in his own deed of one-half of the fishing rights on the Merrimack River, which bounded this land on the west.

In turn, "Samuel Smith of Topsfield . . . gentleman" conveyed one-half interest in his father's farm (Asael had received one-half interest by will from his father) to Asael Smith "of Derryfield . . . cooper," for a recited consideration of 250 pounds on Mar. 24, 1786. Essex County, Mass., Land Records, vol. 145, p. 192. The witnesses and the attesting justice of Essex County, Mass., on the two deeds are the same.

Both deeds are dated Mar. 24, 1786, which correlates with the probate records at the Registry of Probate, Essex County Courthouse, Salem, Mass., File No. 25750. The will was proved Dec. 6, 1785, with the appointment of the committee for appraisal on that day. Their appraisal of Samuel Smith's personal and real property is dated Dec. 20, 1785, and Samuel Smith, Jr., filed this document as executor Feb. 7, 1786. Thus, both sons of Asael were fully aware of the relationship of assets to liabilities in the estate, just as John Smith represents. Personal property of Samuel was valued at about 100 pounds, and land at about 400 pounds, plus receivables, making the total estate's round value 544 pounds. Asael's recited consideration is about half of this sum. Liabilities are not listed.

[148]Assessment Records, Topsfield, Mass., copies of which were furnished by researcher friends Nancy Richards and Robert Yukes. Asael Smith was assessed taxes from 1786 to 1790.

[149]The farming operation was mainly pasture and meadow land, though some eight acres were under cultivation and in orchard. About a dozen each of cattle and sheep were kept, as well as draft animals and a few pigs. Much hay was harvested, and quantities were on hand of grain, potatoes, and flax. This profile is based on the fairly constant itemization of the operation of Samuel Smith, Sr. and Jr., during the years to 1784, after which only total acreage and animals appear in the Topsfield assessments. Asael did not alter the system of production. Cp. n. 124 and n. 156.

[150]John Smith, Journal, July 20, 1839. The bracketed "were" replaces the ms. "was."

[151]Prices fell by as much as 50% in the post-Revolution depression. G. F. Warren, F. A. Pearson, and Herman M. Stoker, *Wholesale Prices for 213 Years, 1720 to 1932, Cornell University Agricultural Experiment Station Memoir,* No. 142 (1932), pp. 7-8; *Statistical History of the United States from Colonial Times to the Present* (Stamford, Conn., [1965]), pp. 116-21. Cp. the tendency of farm prices to correlate with general prices (ibid., p. 112) and Stoker's analysis of the post-war depression lasting about eight years: "It was not until about the latter part of 1792 that a definite recovery in prices was noticeable" (p. 204), a period spanning the entire time that Asael managed the farm. Cp. the specific plight of the Massachusetts farmer: "Thus, the state sought to collect taxes in hard money when virtually none was to be had, and creditors sought to collect debts in hard money at the same time." Merrill Jensen, "The American Revolution and American Agriculture," *Agricultural History,* vol. 43 (1969), p. 120. For general background on the post-war depression, see Oscar Theodore Barck, Jr., and Hugh Talmage Lefler, *Colonial America* (2d. ed.; New York, 1968), pp. 670-71.

[152]For a survey of the rebellion see ibid., pp. 671-73. The hundreds involved in armed resistance symbolized a very general discontent. For details, see Marion L. Starkey, *A Little Rebellion* (New York, 1955).

[153]John Smith's recollections (reproduced in chapter 7) mention the "rent of her third" and the "rent of her land." The stepmother's dower right is mentioned also in the settlement of her own estate: "cash received for rent of her dower part of year." Account of Administration, Estate of Priscilla Smith, June 5, 1798, Essex County, Mass., Registry of Probate, file 25718.

[154]Samuel Smith's will provided living quarters and rights in the home for his widow, giving his real and personal property in equal shares to his sons Samuel and Asael. As Samuel well knew, his widow could exercise her dower right of a life estate in his real property. This took precedence over creditors, and is defined in several statutes.

Dower in Massachusetts was early codified from its common-law background, confirming the right of the widow to "one-third part of all such houses, lands . . . as her husband was seized of . . . to have and enjoy for the term of her natural life, according to the estate of such husband, free and freely discharged of, and from all titles, debts, rents, charges, judgements, executions, and other incumbrances whatsoever, had, made or suffered by her husband during the said marriage between them, or by any other person claiming by, from or under him. . . ." Colonial Laws, 1641, "Dowries," *The Colonial Laws of Massachusetts* (Boston, 1887), p. 42.

In the case of intestacy, debts were subtracted from personal property, but dower was separate: "upon due hearing and consideration thereof (debts, funeral and just expenses of all sorts being first allowed), the said judge shall . . . make a just distribution of the surplusage, or remaining goods and estate as well real as personal, in manner following; that is to say, one-third part of the personal estate to the wife of the intestate forever, besides her dower or thirds in the houses and lands during life. . . ." Province Laws, 1692-3, chap. 14, sec. 1, *Acts and Resolves, Public and Private, of the Province of the Massachusetts Bay* (Boston, 1869).

The intestacy statute operated in the case of renunciation of the will: "Also the widow in all cases may waive the provision made for her in the will of her deceased husband, and claim her dower and have the same assigned her, in the same manner as though her husband had died intestate, in which case she shall receive no benefit from such provision, unless it appears by the will plainly the testator's intention to be in addition to her dower." Mass. Laws, 1783, chap. 24, *Acts and Laws of the Commonwealth of Massachusetts* (Boston,

1890). Cp. the related intestacy provision: "the widow of the deceased shall in all cases be intitled to her dower in the real estate (where she shall not have been otherways endowed before marriage) and to a recovery of the same, in manner as the law directs." ibid., chap. 36.

[155]John Smith, Journal, July 20, 1839. The economic facts support the family tradition of sacrifice for honor:

The only papers in Samuel Smith's probate file are the attested will and inventory indicated in n. 147. Since no distribution documents appear, perhaps Asael dropped further probate proceedings and dealt directly with his father's creditors. The Topsfield farm and related lots were sold Mar. 15, 1791, by "Asael Smith of Topsfield . . . cooper" to "Nathaniel Perkins Averill of Topsfield" for a stated consideration of 270 pounds, about a third less than their value in the inventory of Samuel Smith's estate of 371 pounds. Essex County, Mass., Land Records, vol. 152, p. 224. The difference is evidently the one-third life estate of the widow, as John Smith reports: "He finally sold the farm for what he could get, with the encumbrance of the old lady's third on it."

There is a mistake in copying this 1791 deed, since the basic property (excluding related lots) is described as "a certain farm situate and lying in Topsfield aforesaid (with a dwelling house and barn standing thereon) containing about five acres, more or less. . . ." This is practically identical to the description of the 1786 deed of Samuel, Jr., to Asael (cit. n. 147), but that description reads, "containing about seventy-five acres, more or less. . . ." The metes and bounds descriptions of the two deeds recite the same measurements, so it is evident that the larger amount of land was conveyed, with an accidental omission of "seventy" in the second deed. The 1791 deed to Averill with the mistake of "five acres" recites the same neighbors and bounds as Averill's U. S. tax assessment of 1798, which identifies the farm as 93 acres, which is approximately the same that Asael Smith deeded to him, assuming the correct reading of 75 acres plus the additional lots of land specified. Harriet S. Tapley (ed.), "The United States Direct Tax of 1798, as Assessed on Topsfield," *Historical Collections of . . . Topsfield,* vol. 7 (1901), p. 60.

Cp. the LDS Historian's handwritten but undated manuscript, comparing closely in paper and writing to a similar 1870 biography of Asael Smith, Jr., written while George A. Smith was historian: "His elder brother Samuel relinquished all claim to the property on conditions that Asael would pay the debts and liabilities, which he found the property insufficient to do, himself paying out of his own means about $700 to close the accounts rather than to endure the disgrace of having his father's estate entered upon the records as insolvent."

In terms of financial realities, Asael traded land to move to the Topsfield farm (n. 147); from 1786 to 1791 he used the farm's profits to pay "some part of his father's debts"; then John Smith indicates that the final sale of land went almost entirely for Samuel Smith's creditors. What Asael had to pay can be estimated from the estate inventory (n. 147), the deed of sale cited in this note, and John Smith's history. John says that the debts exceeded the value of the estate, inventoried at 544 pounds. Asael realized 270 pounds from selling the farm. If this amount paid off the creditors, then he had already paid 274 pounds on the total indebtedness, a little more than the $700 mentioned in the LDS Historian's document. This does not count the value of the farm that Asael traded to his brother in coming to Topsfield. He obviously came out with little left, as John Smith says, for he rented for a time, and then paid only 26 pounds for his uncleared farm in Vermont (n. 170).

[156]Rev. A. P. Putnam, "Danvers, at Home and Abroad," No. 60, *Danvers* [Mass.] *Mirror,* Sept. 19, 1885. Putnam prefaces his quotation with the source of the assessment poem: "Asael, son of Samuel and grandfather of 'Joe' could write a very good letter, and it would seem that he was occasionally, not to say frequently, inclined to let his thoughts run to rhymes. Among the scraps found on file in the archives of this town, is one that is traced with the following lives [lines] in the former poet's own handwriting." The beginning installment of this series on Topsfield (No. 58, Aug. 29, 1885) indicated, "This summer I am fortunate enough to have my vacation home in the quiet, but very pleasant and beautiful old historic town of Topsfield." Subsequent comments indicated his close association with John H. Gould, the clerk of Topsfield, who showed him the poem under discussion, as well as the Jacob Towne, Jr., letter of Asael Smith and the Humphrey Gould correspondence of George A. Smith. Since these last items are quoted with care, there is no doubt regarding the basic accuracy of the assessment rhyme, though the location of the original is unknown since Putnam examined it.

Putnam was a responsible author and a competent local historian, publishing dozens of articles in the *Danvers Mirror.* For a convenient biography, see *Biographical Review, Containing Life Sketches of Leading Citizens of Essex County, Massachusetts* (Boston, 1898), pp. 159-61. Spelling has been corrected in the following instances: "pole" (corrected to poll to make clear its reference to the poll tax), "Stears," "heffer," "grone," "sarch," "you'le." Putnam's article was only found because of early family historian Edith A. Smith's naming Putnam, and the diligence of Robert Yukes in searching the *Danvers Mirror* for the correct installment.

Having two poll assessments would date the poem 1786 to 1791, when his sons were mature. Two polls are listed in the Topsfield tax records in 1787, 1789, and 1790. The animals listed do not quite correspond in two of those years, though the full listing is not available in 1787. However, the poem gives an approximation of his property in these years. For instance, in 1789 he inventoried 4 cows, 2 two-year-old steers, 3 yearlings, 3 two-year-old heifers, and 2 swine. Up to that year he was taxed on 90 acres of land, which increased to 96½ in 1790—unimproved land or woodland might account for the discrepancy between the 82 acres of the poem and the amounts on the Topsfield assessment records. I am indebted to Nancy Richards for taking time to copy these records.

[157]Several Mormon histories allege that Asael Smith was forced to leave Topsfield because of sheltering a Quaker, although Joseph Fielding Smith's careful historical works do not mention this. Asael's grandson George A. Smith applied a similar tradition not to Asael, but to a common ancestor of the Smiths and Goulds, who united when Asael's father, Samuel, married Priscilla Gould. Writing to Humphrey Gould (June 6, 1870), George A. spoke of one ancestor who sheltered a Quaker, and also John Gould, early political dissenter: "It was no doubt a grave offence to entertain Quakers in the days of our venerable ancestor; yet now we feel a pride that he was so liberal minded. We admire that hatred of oppression which prompted Capt. John Gould to freely express his views in contempt of Sir Edmund Andros, the tyrannical governor." These comments were in response to Humphrey Gould's letter to George A. Smith of May 26, 1870 (from Rowe, Mass.), mentioning John Gould's criticism of "Edmund Andros, the hateful, tyrannical governor of Massachusetts"—and commenting on the prominence of John's father, Zaccheus Gould, in early records: "Again in 1659 as a criminal. What, our noble ancestor a criminal? Verily so. He was fined three (3) pounds for harboring Quakers. They were kindred from Rhode Island."

So George A. Smith's "grave offence to entertain Quakers" clearly refers to John Gould's father, Zaccheus Gould, who in 1659 was fined three pounds for housing his Quaker nephew Daniel Gould, who in turn was sentenced to whipping and ordered to leave the area. Zaccheus Gould's fine was remitted six months later "in consequence of his great loss lately sustained by fire." Primary and secondary sources of this episode are surveyed in Benjamin Apthorp Gould, *The Family of Zaccheus Gould of Topsfield* (Lynn, Mass., 1895), pp. 31-32, the work evidently relied on for the abbreviated account in Dow, *History of Topsfield,* p. 26.

John Smith's very detailed history of moving from Topsfield to Vermont (reproduced in chapter 7) gives no hint of Asael's leaving Topsfield for sheltering a Quaker. Perhaps the tradition arose by an incorrect reading of Rev. A. P. Putnam's comment after quoting Asael's assessment poem at Topsfield: "It is hardly to be inferred that one who was thus open and explicit was finally driven into the wilds of New Hampshire by any oppressive treatment on the part of the people here; yet true it is that he led his family out of the fertile region of *'New Meadows'* into the more sterile lands of the Granite State." *Danvers Mirror,* Sept. 19, 1885. Putnam's point is the same one made in this chapter—that Asael was obviously well accepted and had no apparent reason for leaving Topsfield. He was puzzled by not knowing the true circumstances. Incidentally, Putnam reversed Asael's New Hampshire residence, incorrectly thinking that it immediately followed the Topsfield move.

[158]Perhaps the best insight to Jacob Towne, Jr., comes from his personal acquaintance Dr. Cleaveland: "I should do injustice to this name, if I should omit to mention here, the late Jacob Towne, Esq., of Topsfield. For years—I know not how many—this excellent individual held the offices of town clerk, selectman, and representative to the General Court, until he came, at length, to be regarded as a sort of personification of his beloved Topsfield. He was the calmest, the most deliberate, the most cautious of men. If he ever uttered a hasty word, or did a rash act, I never heard of it. If ever there were a true conservative, it was Jacob Towne, Jr. He, alas, is gone. But it is some consolation that, faithful to the ancient rule and privilege of primogeniture, he transmitted so large a share of his own careful spirit to the present custodian of the Topsfield archives." Nehemiah Cleaveland, *Address Delivered at Topsfield, in Massachusetts, Aug. 28, 1850* (New York, 1851), p. xxvii.

The son alluded to by Cleaveland is J. Perkins Towne, Topsfield clerk who had possession of the 1796 letter of Asael to Jacob Towne, Jr., when visited by George A. Smith in 1872: "I am also under obligation to . . . the town clerk of that place, Mr. Towne, for valuable letters and papers relating to the history of our family. George A. Smith, *Journal of Discourses,* vol. 15 (Liverpool, 1873), p. 97 (discourse of July 7, 1872). This letter was immediately published in the *Deseret News,* July 16, 1872. For Jacob P. Towne's term as town clerk, 1836-1878, see *History of Essex County, Massachusetts* (Philadelphia, 1888), vol. 2, p. 984.

Asael Smith's friend Jacob Towne, Jr., was town clerk, 1810-1836; selectman, 1799-1800, 1803-1805, 1811-1813, 1815, 1818-1822; and representative to the Mass. legislature 1827-1835 (ibid., pp. 984-87). Towne (1768-1836) was younger than Asael, and his parents, to whom Asael sends regards, were slightly older than Asael. George Francis Dow, "Pine Grove Cemetery Inscriptions," *Historical Collections of . . . Topsfield,* vol. 7 (1901), p. 31. Cp. *Vital Records of Topsfield,* p. 253. Basic sketches of the lives of Jacob Towne, his son Jacob Towne, Jr., and his son Jacob Perkins Towne are found in Edwin Eugene Towne, *Descendants of William Towne* (Newtonville, Mass., 1901), pp. 36, 57, 99.

[159]Topsfield's economic profile appears just two years after Asael's letter in the records of the United States direct tax of 1798 (so cited in subsequent footnotes), copied from Boston archives and published in the *Historical Collections of . . . Topsfield,* vol. 7 (1901). Both Jacob Towne, Jr., and his father had their own homes, productive farms (68 and 57 acres), barns (plus the son's cider mill), and grazing land (p. 86). For the personal profile of this warm and intelligent family, see the extensive correspondence preserved in the *Historical Collections of . . . Topsfield,* vol. 18 (1913), pp. 10 ff.

[160]Dr. John Merriam (1758-1817) was one of two doctors in Topsfield during Asael Smith's residence. He began practice there in 1783, according to his associate, Dr. Nehemiah Cleaveland, who quotes a complimentary tribute to his honesty. *Address,* p. xx (cit. n. 158). Dow's detailed life sketch comments on his capacity: "He was an old time physician with a considerable practice. It is said of him that he was well prepared for the work of his profession, as the times then were. His medical library was large for those days. From entries made in his own handwriting in books of his library it would appear that his studies preparatory to the study of medicine were considerable, and that he had some knowledge of Latin. . . . From

what we learn of him it is certain that he stood high as a medical practitioner, and he had the respect of his patrons and of the community in general. He had a large practice that extended into the adjoining towns. *History of Topsfield,* pp. 424-25.

Cp. the letter of Solomon Wildes to Dr. John Merriam, Boston, Feb. 9, 1793, reporting (at Dr. Merriam's request) the prices of books for sale there. *Historical Collections of . . . Topsfield,* vol. 18 (1913), p. 27.

[161]On Joseph Cree, see U. S. direct tax of 1798 (cit. n. 159) and Dow, *History of Topsfield,* p. 358.

[162]The Topsfield deeds already discussed from Samuel and Asael Smith describe their property as bounding the Dormans'. Also the U. S. direct tax of 1798 identifies the property of the purchaser of the Smith farm (Nathaniel Perkins Averill) as holding land next to that of Ephraim and Joseph Dorman. Ephraim appears to be an uncle of Joseph Dorman, whose father Nathaniel died in 1776. When Asael sent regards, neighbor Joseph Dorman would have been about 29. *Vital Records of Topsfield,* pp. 35, 217.

[163]Jacob Towne's personal accounts (cit. n. 159) show entries paying Charles Rogers "for picking rocks" (May 28, 1793) and settling "in full, 15/6d" (Nov. 21, 1795).

[164]*Journal of Discourses* vol. 15 (Liverpool, 1873), p. 69 (discourse of July 8, 1872). Humphrey Gould was born in 1797 (six years after Asael's move from Topsfield) and stated regarding Asael Smith: "I remember when a very small boy seeing him sitting at my father's table. He was a wry necked man, which fact attracted my attention." Letter to George A. Smith, May 2, 1870, Rowe, Mass. Cp. n. 183.

[165]Asael and two sons signed a note to "Thomas Emerson of Topsfield" for seven hundred dollars payable in one year, made June 1, 1803, with an accompanying mortgage. Tunbridge, Vt., Land Records, vol. 3, p. 69. Emerson released his interest to Jesse Smith Sept. 13, 1805, for $800 consideration. Ibid., vol. 3, p. 358. Emerson owned more land and buildings than anyone in Topsfield, measured by the U. S. direct tax of 1798, cit. n. 159.

[166]The foregoing references are taken from John Smith's Journal, July 20, 1839.

[167]Letter of George A. Smith to Humphrey Gould, June 10, 1870, Salt Lake City, in which he refers to "a little incident that I

heard my father relate." Cp. Dow, *History of Topsfield,* p. 362, which copies the minutes of "a meeting held by the carpenters, housewrights, and wheelwrights of the Town of Topsfield," Feb. 28, 1793, at which "Mr. Elijah Averill was chosen moderator." Cp. Jacob Towne's account entry of Mar. 11, 1795, paying "Elijah Averell for putting in an axletree." *Historical Collections of . . . Topsfield,* vol. 18 (1913), p. 30. George Francis Dow gives Elijah Averill's vital dates (1762-1813) and calls him a "housewright." "William Averill of Ipswich and Some of His Descendants," ibid., vol. 17 (1912), p. 77.

[168]Massachusetts records show the Topsfield farm was sold Mar. 15, 1791 (cit. n. 155). Vermont records show the purchase of the Tunbridge farm June 21, 1791 (cit. n. 170). The Topsfield assessments contain Asael Smith until 1790, but on May 30, 1791, appraise the same property in the name of "Nathaniel Perkins Averell," the purchaser from Asael. In turn, in the Tunbridge, Vt., Town Record is "a list of freemen sworn," with the dates of admission into town affairs—Asael is entered in 1792. Finally, Asael Smith's letter from Tunbridge, Jan. 14, 1796 (reproduced in chapter 6), speaks of his farm as "but four years occupied," which fits the late 1791 move of John Smith's account, with an earlier purchase verified by the Vermont deed.

[169]John Smith, Journal, July 20, 1839. Although "Asahel" is the spelling of the brother's name in this passage, John lists him at the beginning of the document as "Asael." Cp. notes 122, 174, 233.

[170]Tunbridge, Vt., Land Records, vol. 1, p. 324 (June 21, 1791). Consideration was 26 pounds for about 83 acres, just about the dollar per acre that John Smith remembered. Journal, July 20, 1839. This land appreciated rapidly on being cleared and farmed.

[171]Letter of Asael Smith to Jacob Towne, Jr., Jan. 14, 1796, Tunbridge, Vt. See chapter 6 for the reproduction of this letter, the manuscript of which is at Essex Institute, Salem, Mass. I am indebted to Miss Nancy Richards for locating the original. Cp. the early publication of this letter by George A. Smith, who obtained a copy from Topsfield. *Deseret News,* July 16, 1872 (n. 158).

[172]The original purchase of lot 18 (n. 170) was increased by acquiring title to the 100 acres of lot 17 from two grantors: Tunbridge, Vt., Land Records, vol. 2, p. 121 (Nov. 29, 1794); vol. 3, p. 75 (Sept. 4, 1801). The additional 100 acres of lot 10 were acquired Dec. 17, 1795; Tunbridge, Vt., Land Records, vol. 2, p. 211.

Possible partnerships appear in the conveyance just mentioned of Sept. 4, 1801, in which title is taken by Asael and Silas Smith, and also in Silas' conveyance of this one-half interest to Asael Smith, Jr. (Asael, Sr., holding the other half), on July 9, 1803. Tunbridge, Vt., Land Records, vol. 3, p. 304.

[173]Jesse Smith's first recorded deed is the purchase of the 100-acre lot 19, on Nov. 19, 1794. John Smith's recollection (reproduced in chapter 7) was that his father had given Jesse "50 acres of land" out of a total 183 acres of initial purchase in 1791. Title was only taken to 83 acres in 1791 (n. 170), but Jesse's 100 acres could well have been occupied under a contract to purchase in 1791.

[174]Tunbridge Town Record, p. 233. Asael's son's name appears as "Asahel" here, a tendency in family records, though the autograph on the letter of June 24, 1843 (Nashville, Iowa, to the President of the Twelve), is spelled "Asael." Cp. n. 169.

[175]Tunbridge Town Record, pp. 73-74 (bridge committee, 1793), p. 80 (selectman and moderator, 1793), p. 86 (selectman and petit juror, 1794), p. 88 (committee on meetinghouse, 1794), p. 200 (end of selectman term, 1795), p. 220 (grand juror, 1798), p. 255 (highway surveyor, 1802). Several other references mention Asael in the exercise of the above offices.

[176]Lucy Smith, preliminary manuscript, the equivalent of *Biographical Sketches*, p. 37, where Lucy outlines her stay with Stephen Mack some two years prior to her marriage in early 1796. Cp. the chart "A Chronology for the Mack Sisters," pp. 68-69.

Asael Smith and Stephen Mack both signed a petition as prominent citizens of Tunbridge on Oct. 13, 1794. Allen Soule (ed.), *State Papers of Vermont,* vol. 10, General Petitions, 1793-1796 (Montpelier, 1958), pp. 83-84.

[177]Asael Smith to Towne, Jan. 14, 1796, cit. n. 171.

[178]William Smith's editorial note in the *Wasp* (Nauvoo, Ill.), June 11, 1842: "MORMON CREED. To mind their own business, and let everybody else *do likewise.*" This "Mormon Creed" was occasionally mentioned in pioneer Utah speeches.

[179]George A. Smith to Humphrey Gould, May 31, 1870, Salt Lake City. This letter describes Asael Smith's notations in the pamphlet: "I received from my grandfather Asael Smith a pamphlet entitled a 'Caution to Great Britain and Her Colonies,' in which he wrote his name several times as 'Asael Smith, his hand.' He has also

entered on a blank leaf the names and dates of birth of several of his children. . . . Under Asael Smith's name in the pamphlet before mentioned is written the following: 'Steal not this book / For fear of shame / For over this is the / owner's name.' " George A. Smith later copied Asael's notation of date of purchase of the same pamphlet. On the "flyleaf" was written: " 'Asael Smith, his book, bought 1772.' Over the leaf is again written: 'Asael Smith, his book, May the first 1772.' " So Asael had kept the work almost 60 years when presented to George A. Smith. G. A. Smith to Gould, June 10, 1870.

[180]Anthony Benezet, *A Caution and Warning to Great Britain and Her Colonies* (Philadelphia, 1767), p. 1. Although Asael's copy has not been located, George A. Smith identified the edition: "The pamphlet contains 52 pages, and is a strong remonstrance against English slavery of the Africans by 'Anthony Benezet,' 'Philadelphia, printed by D. Hall and W. Sellers, at the New Printing Office, in Market Street. MDCCLXVII.' " G. A. Smith to Gould, May 31, 1870. Although George A. Smith evidently left out "and Warning" from the title, all other particulars correspond to entry 10555 in Charles Evans, *American Bibliography* (reprint; New York, 1941), vol. 4, p. 86, from which the quotation is taken.

[181]Asael Smith to Towne, Jan. 14, 1796.

[182]In 1850 Nehemiah Cleaveland said of Asael Smith: "This man, like 'Ammon's great son, one shoulder had too high,' and thence usually bore the significant and complimentary designation of 'Crook-necked Smith.' He was so free in his opinions on religious subjects that some regarded his sentiments as more distorted than his neck." *An Address Delivered at Topsfield, in Massachusetts, August 28, 1850: The Two Hundredth Anniversary of the Incorporation of the Town* (New York, 1851), p. xxv. Cleaveland was a physician who settled in Topsfield in 1783 and thus was practicing during Asael's second stay there from 1786 to 1791. Ibid., p. 46. Cleaveland was acquainted with Asael Smith, for he was the justice of the peace before whom Asael and Mary Smith acknowledged a 1791 deed of sale. Essex County Land Records, vol. 152, p. 224. How well Cleaveland knew Asael is another matter, since he does not give his own direct opinion; furthermore, Cleaveland appears to have been highly orthodox himself. See Charles J. Peabody, "A Sketch of Dr. Nehemiah Cleaveland," *Historical Collections of . . . Topsfield*, vol. 1 (1895), p. 35 ff. Asael's theological orthodoxy is criticized, not his Christian devotion.

[183]G. A. Smith to Gould, May 31, 1870, in which the author speculates on the loss of these writings: "I could never get hold of them. I think they must have been suppressed by Uncle Jesse, who was a covenanter, lived near him and visited him nearly every day during his last illness." Cp. n. 201.

Incidentally, about 1803 Asael strongly disapproved of Methodism, perhaps because of its vigorous preaching of the eternal condemnation of the unregenerate. Lucy Smith, *Biographical Sketches*, p. 54. Lucy's preliminary manuscript here adds the further detail of Asael Smith's demonstrating disapproval of the Methodist interest of his son Joseph Smith, Sr. Asael "came to the door one day and threw Tom Paine's *Age of Reason* into the house and angrily bade him read that until he believed it." Asael Smith by no means agreed with Paine's theology, however, for the *Age of Reason* ridicules the divinity of Christ, the atonement, the resurrection, and the authenticity of the New Testament, all of which Asael deeply accepted, as shown in his family address (chapter 6), written about this time. His act may have been scornful, an association of the then unpopular Methodism with the deviations of Paine—or an agreement with Paine's attack on religious superstition, though Asael Smith stopped far short of the extremism of the *Age of Reason.*

No direct source is known for the cause of Asael Smith's "awry" neck, though descendant Joseph Fielding Smith perhaps had access to either family tradition or written information in saying that "he was not deformed in any way, but while a small child his neck was severely burned, which caused the cords to contract, making his neck stiff." "Asael Smith of Topsfield," p. 90. Cp. n. 164.

[184]Profession of Faith of the General Convention of Universalists, 1803. Winchester, N. H., cit. Rev. A. B. Grosh, "Universalists," I. Daniel Rupp, *An Original History of the Religious Denominations* (Philadelphia, 1844), p. 727.

[185]Tunbridge Town Record, p. 188 (Dec. 6, 1797), with one signer subtracted because of his noted disclaimer. The episode reveals Asael's broad theology but must not be exaggerated, since he shortly appears as a pew holder in the town meeting house (p. 196), and the Universalist exemption is related to a compromise in assessments in building it. Similarly, he had been assigned seating in the Topsfield meeting house in 1762. "The Seating in the Meeting House, 1762 and 1771," *Historical Collections of . . . Topsfield*, vol. 7 (1901), p. 94; also cit. Dow, *History of Topsfield*, p. 256. As

pointed out, his first children had been baptized in the Congregational Church at Topsfield (n. 129). Cp. his son's universalism, n. 205.

[186]Quotations following are from Asael Smith's Address to His Family. The text cited is that of the original at the LDS Historian's Office. Its first publication was by Joseph Fielding Smith, "Asahel Smith of Topsfield." A complete photographic reproduction appears in chapter 6.

[187]See Mack, *Narrative*, pp. 20-21, where Solomon Mack confessed accepting the "universal principle" during "the early part of my life," though he finally felt that it encouraged "false hopes," in part a reflection of his own experience of delaying serious religious decision.

[188]Asael Smith, Address to His Family, the source of unnoted quotations running back to n. 186, which gives the full citation.

[189]Ibid. (cp. n. 126).

[190]Ibid.

[191]A summary of the extended Revolutionary service of Mary's three brothers is given in Anderson, *Ancestry and Posterity*, p. 116, which however is inaccurate regarding Mary's sisters.

The physical prowess of one sister appears in the following early and basically correct recollection: "Dec. 4: John Merrill came here and says that William Duty, who resided on our place, was a very courageous man. He was in the Bunker Hill fight and stood close by Maj. McClary of Chichester when a four pound ball struck him in the back and killed him. William Duty had a sister Eunice, who could take up a barrel of cider and drink out of the bung—also a sister who was the wife of William Rowell of Salem; children: Washington, James, Moses Duty, Polly (who mar. Alfred Snell), Levina (who is widow of Jona. Rowell), and William (who mar. a Merrill and had children)." Alfred Poore, "A Genealogical-Historical Visitation of Groveland, Mass., in the Year 1863," *Historical Collections of the Essex Institute,* vol. 55 (1919), p. 241. See n. 127 for Mary Duty's family, including her father's will, which names daughter Hannah Duty. The town record of Salem, N. H., records the marriage of William Rowell and Hannah Duty, June 6, 1776. State copy, vol. 2, p. 627. Marriages of children Levina and William are also verified in the Salem, N. H., town record. Ibid., vol. 5, pp. 415, 471.

[192]John Smith, Journal, July 20, 1839. The recollection is from the impressionable age of ten, when John was left to help his mother with the Ipswich dairy operation while his father and older brothers established a new residence in Vermont.

[193]The beginning of John Smith's narrative (ibid., reproduced in chapter 7) gives the names of the eleven children, and their birth-dates appear in Asael Smith's family Bible: Jesse (Apr. 20, 1768), Priscilla (Oct. 21, 1769), Joseph, Sr. (July 12, 1771), Asael, Jr. (May 21, 1773), Mary (June 4, 1775), Samuel (Sept. 15, 1777), Silas (Oct. 1, 1779), John (July 16, 1781), Susan (May 18, 1783), Stephen (Apr. 23, 1785), Sarah (May 16, 1789). Most of these dates are also entered in the Derryfield, N. H., town book in Asael Smith's handwriting. Cp. notes 128, 129, 140, and 201. Brief biographies and some vital dates appear in Joseph Fielding Smith, "Asahel Smith of Topsfield," pp. 97-101.

[194]The Tunbridge Town Record has about two dozen entries on Jesse Smith between 1796 and 1810, most of them offices to which he was elected.

[195]Lucy Smith's record of her early marriage in *Biographical Sketches* describes these careers, including that of merchandising.

[196]Family information beyond church offices comes from the historical sketch of Asael Smith, Jr., sent to Humphrey Gould by George A. Smith, May 28, 1870, Salt Lake City. Judge Elias Smith, son of Asael, Jr., may have been consulted in composing this bio-graphy. George A. Smith's opinion of his Uncle Asael was given earlier in a letter reporting his death:

"President Asael Smith, brother to the aged patriarch Joseph Smith, died at Iowaville, Wappelo Co., Iowa, on the 22d July, 1848, aged 75 years and two months. He was a strong advocate for the Book of Mormon in 1830 and has been a firm supporter of the cause of Zion ever since—and his days were shortened by exposure to cruelty and mob violence. He was ordained a patriarch in 1844. His principles, precepts, and examples were worthy of imitation, and shed a lustre that does honor to his high and holy calling. He died of a long and painful illness, and has left a numerous family to mourn his loss." George A. Smith to Orson Pratt, Oct. 20, 1848, Council Bluffs [Iowa], *Latter-day Saints' Millenial Star,* vol. 11 (1849), p. 13.

[197]Jesse N. Smith, youngest son of Silas, surveyed his father's life in the beginning of his journal, recording the family tradition

of service in the War of 1812, and summarizing his father's ordinations to the office of elder (Mar. 3, 1836, Kirtland, Ohio) and of high priest (Feb. 10, 1838, Kirtland, Ohio), based on certificates. He died after hardships of the Missouri expulsion, on Sept. 13, 1839.

[198]John Smith's extensive 1854 obituary appears at the beginning of chapter 7.

[199]*The Weekly Wanderer* (Randolph, Vt.), Aug. 14, 1802. This death notice was partially prompted by the Smiths' desire to clear the attending physician from blame in Stephen's death. The second paragraph and remaining part of the obituary is as follows: "It is reported that Dr. Joseph Tuffs (who was desired to visit the above deceased in his last moments) gave something under pretence to relieve him, which proved or seemed to hasten him out of the world, which report is infamous and absolutely false. The parents of the deceased and one brother, who were present at the time and till the young man died, are ready, if called upon, to testify that whoever propagates such a story is guilty of the most infamous slander and detraction, and that no truth is attached to it, but the reverse."

[200]Lovejoy, *History of Royalton,* pp. 317-18, which also indicates a regular term in the year 1803-04.

[201]Several family records of Asael Smith's descendants evidently copy a detailed record of family dates once in Asael's possession, containing first-person notations of himself and his father. This may be the "large book of Grandfather Asahel Smith's writings" that the family of son Silas Smith was forced to leave in Illinois, as Jesse N. Smith mentions toward the beginning of his journal. Son John Smith copied the family record in his large journal, pp. 100-105, headed, "copy of a journal kept by my grandfather, Asael Smith—a similar record exists in the notebook of Don Carlos Smith, son of Joseph Smith, Sr. This record is also copied by George A. Smith on pages added to Asael Smith's Bible.

Jesse married Hannah Peabody Jan. 20, 1792, and Joseph married Lucy Mack Jan. 24, 1796. That year Priscilla was joined to John C. Waller (Aug. 24) and Mary to Isaac Pierce (Dec. 22). These last marriages and the prominence of the Waller and Pierce families are noted in Lovejoy, *History of Royalton,* pp. 909, 1013.

The marriage of Asael, Jr., to Betsy Shellinger "of Royalton" Mar. 21, 1802, is noted in John Smith's copy of Asael's record and also in the Royalton town records. Four years later Silas also married a Royalton girl, Ruth Stevens. The fathers of these women were Abraham Schellinger and Abel Stevens, both of which are mentioned in Lovejoy, *History of Royalton.* After Betsy Schellinger died, Asael, Jr., was remarried (in New York) to schoolteacher Mary Aikens (Mar. 4, 1828). Mary and her parents were from New England, and after Silas' death in 1839 she gave determined moral leadership to her family, as related by her son Jesse N. Smith in his autobiography, *Journal of Jesse Nathaniel Smith* (Salt Lake City, 1953).

The Lyman family into which John Smith married is well known in Mormon records. See also Lyman Coleman, *Genealogy of the Lyman Family* (Albany, 1872). John married Clarissa Lyman Sept. 11, 1815.

[202]George A. Smith, *Journal of Discourses,* vol. 5 (Liverpool, 1858), p. 101 (Aug. 2, 1857, discourse). Cp. the sketch of Asael Smith, Jr., sent by George A. Smith to Humphrey Gould, May 31, 1870: "He possessed a remarkable memory, was a thorough student of the scriptures, which he was ever ready to repeat, and it was a saying among his nephews that Uncle Asael could read the Bible as well without the book as with."

[203]George A. Smith, "Memoirs," opening section.

[204]John Smith, Journal, Aug. 20, 1836.

[205]Although the universalism of Joseph Smith, Sr., has been noted above, this was a philosophy, not commitment to that organized movement. His wife emphasizes that "he would not subscribe to any particular system of faith, but contended for the ancient order as established by our Lord and Savior Jesus Christ and his apostles." *Biographical Sketches,* pp. 56-57. Lucy also reports his profound searching that resulted in several impressive dreams on his religious duties. For the father's universalism, cp. n. 185.

[206]In 1824 married sister Sarah Smith Sanford died and was buried beside Stephen at Royalton, Vermont. In early May 1830, another brother, Samuel, died. St. Lawrence County Probate Records, Canton, N. Y., Surrogate's File No. 304.

John Smith is the main source of the attitudes of eldest brother Jesse and the three remaining sisters. His daily journal entries of the 1836 mission have been preserved, as well as a summary narrative in the first person, published in Lucy Smith, *Biographical Sketches,* p. 214. Combining the two accounts, one learns that in or near Lebanon, N. H., they visited "sister Pierce" (Mary) also called "a own sister, whom we had not seen for twenty years." Very prejudiced against the message of her brothers, she began "to hear a little today," but was evidently far from fully believing.

In St. Lawrence County, N. Y., John tells of rejection by Jesse, after which they "came to Potsdam; found sister Susan well but full of popularity and pride." Later George A. Smith's cousin informed him that Susan had not married, but had cared for her deceased sister's child: "Your father's sister Susan lived and died a maiden lady; and her adopted daughter Charlotte Sanford followed her example. These facts came to me through acquaintance in P[otsdam]." Letter of Hannah P. Butler to George A. Smith, Feb. 25, 1869, South Colton, New York. Susan's estate records indicate her death Mar. 22, 1849; her will is signed "Susan Smith" and names "my niece Charlotte M. Sanford" as sole heir. St. Lawrence County, N. Y., Probate Records, Canton, N. Y., File No. 881. Charlotte was evidently the daughter of Susan's youngest sister, Sarah, who married Joseph Sanford but died in 1824.

Without formally accepting, "our oldest sister . . . was very much pleased to see us, and received our testimony"; John Smith tells of visiting Priscilla Waller in Middlebury, Vt., where they were "well treated" and parted with "our sister in tears." Priscilla was the last-surviving child of Asael, and her belief in Mormonism continued: "Of my grandfather's family there is but one living—an old lady by the name of Waller, residing in the city of New York. And she is 90 years of age and remembers all that has transpired during the last eighty years just as well as if it had all just occurred. I visited her when I was last back there, and in talking with me she would talk of things that had transpired many years back as though they had occurred within a year. She is sanguine in relation to the truth of 'Mormonism,' although she has never embraced it. And, to use the language of her son, she preaches it all the time." George A. Smith, *Journal of Discourses,* vol. 5 (Liverpool, 1858), p. 102 (Aug. 2, 1857, discourse). Cp. the letter of Calvin C. Waller to John Smith, Feb. 28, 1846, New York City, N. Y., which states, "I write you at the request of mother," expresses indignation at the martyrdom of Joseph and Hyrum Smith, and requests news "which you think mother would like to hear."

[207]An interesting trace of his Vermont residence is Asael's notation in the family Bible: "And I Asael Smith was born March the 7th, 1744 . . . and am now in my 62 year and live in Tunbridge, in the State of Vermont, it being the 21 day of April, 1805." His grandson Joseph Smith, Jr., was born later that year.

[208]Only heads of households were named in early censuses, though all individuals appear by sex and age. In 1800 Asael is

named in Tunbridge, and this is clearly Asael, Sr., since he and his wife are listed as 45 and over. In 1810, age also identifies Asael, Sr., at Tunbridge, since he and wife are the only ones in their household, and both 45 and over. Asael and Mary are also identifiable at Stockholm, St. Lawrence County, N. Y., in 1820, since Asael, Jr., and Asael, Sr. are separately listed as heads of households, and the latter 45 and older, living with a woman of the same age bracket. Lucy Smith (*Biographical Sketches,* pp. 154-55) indicates that Asael, Sr., and Mary Duty Smith were living with Silas at Stockholm in 1830, and the census agrees, listing two in his household in the 80-90 age group, one male and one female.

[209]Asael, Sr., and eldest son Jesse evidently migrated to New York last, since they remain at Tunbridge, Vt., in the 1810 census. An LDS Historian's Office manuscript entitled "Biography of John Smith, Patriarch" (dated in pencil May 1854) relates circumstances of the family move to New York, though the handwriting is not identified and all details are not verified. According to this document, Jesse attempted to prevent his brother Silas from possessing a part of his father's property, and the younger brothers moved west rather than cause a dispute. John and Asael, Jr., moved to St. Lawrence County first, and Silas followed, according to this source, which mentions buying land on contract.

No deeds can be located regarding these moves (undoubtedly because land was held under contracts), but two St. Lawrence County, N. Y., sources help on this problem. The 1810 federal census enumerates Asael Smith, Jr. ("Asel Smith"), at Stockholm and Silas Smith at Potsdam. Silas' children correspond to his family of this date, but besides the parents, there are two additional male adults and one additional female adult in the household. These might be the then unmarried brothers Samuel and John, and possibly unmarried sister Susan (Susanna).

The other St. Lawrence County source is an 1815 assessment record of Potsdam, copies of which were furnished by the courtesy of Mary H. Biondi, St. Lawrence County Historian, whose services have been valuable. The following Smiths appear, with notations on their first arrival in the county. Samuel, born 1777, came Aug. 31, 1810; John came Nov. 13, 1810; Silas came Oct. 24, 1806. The above dates of arrival must be treated with caution, however, since their firsthand nature is not clear. George A. Smith had 1809 as the time of Silas' arrival in St. Lawrence County. George A. Smith, "Historical Sketch of Ashael Smith, Son of Asael." This same year was evidently the tradition of the descendants of Silas who remained in St. Lawrence County. *Genealogical and Family History of Northern New York* (New York, 1919), vol. 3, p. 929. By 1820 the father Asael and son Jesse had joined the northern New York pioneers.

[210]The relatively late migration of Asael Smith, Sr., discounts the claim of some county histories that Asael was associated with the cooperative economic settlement of William Bullard. The earliest county history was published when the memory of this settlement was alive, and it associates none of the Asael Smith family with Bullard's group, which took title to land in 1804. Franklin B. Hough, *History of St. Lawrence and Franklin Counties, New York* (Albany, 1853), pp. 435 ff. Land records show partition of the property of the cooperative in 1810. *History of St. Lawrence, Co., New York* (Philadelphia, 1878), p. 240. As discussed in notes 207, 208, and 209, Asael Smith, Sr., was still in Vermont at this time. The burials of Asael Smith's family in St. Lawrence County are separated from Bullard's "Union," and the census enumeration indicates separate areas also.

[211]George A. Smith, "Memoirs," handwritten ms., p. 2, where the episode is dated and described as narrated here. Though an early teenager when these events took place, George A. Smith was unusually mature and took special interest in his grandfather, who gave him the family records in the anti-slavery pamphlet and in the family Bible. He remembered his grandfather's comment on their relationship: "George A. is a rather singular boy. When he comes here, instead of going to play as the rest of my grandchildren do, he comes into my room and asks me questions about what occurred seventy or eighty years ago." George A. Smith, *Journal of Discourses*, vol. 15 (Liverpool, 1873), p. 97 (July 7, 1872, discourse). Cp. G. A. Smith to Gould, May 31, 1870, p. 4: "The reason he assigned for giving me the old family Bible was, that while the other children were off to play, I would come and sit beside him and listen to his narrations and ask questions about history. I was 13 years old at the time of his death and had visited him about three months previously."

[212]George A. Smith, *Journal of Discourses*, vol. 5 (Liverpool, 1858), p. 102 (Aug. 2, 1857, discourse). This is another description of Asael's reaction to the first news of Joseph Smith's visions in 1828.

[213]Letter of Jesse Smith to "Hiram Smith," June 17, 1829, Stockholm [New York], cit. Joseph Smith Letter Book, part 2, pp.

59-60. I have changed "Asahel," a spelling frequently used for Asael, Jr., to "Asael" for consistency.

[214]John Smith, Journal, cited Lucy Smith, *Biographical Sketches,* p. 155.

[215]George A. Smith, "Memoirs," handwritten ms., p. 2.

[216]Ibid.; a similar report is given at the location cit. n. 212.

[217]Further details of Asael Smith's conversion to Mormonism and his death are found in a notebook copying first-person journal entries from the Smith family, the following from a daughter-in-law who lived near Asael, apparently John Smith's wife: "[F]ather Asael Smith . . . on his deathbed declared his full and firm belief in the everlasting gospel and also regretted that he was not baptized when Joseph his son was there and acknowledged that the doctrine of universalism, which he had so long advocated, was not true. For although he had lived by this religion 50 years, yet he now renounced it as insufficient to comfort him in death." M. Wilford Poulson (ed.), "Copy of an Old Notebook," Brigham Young University typescript, pp. 40-41. Cp. n. 224. Professor Poulson's photographs of the original notebook conform to the typescript. They are furnished me by close friend Chad Flake, BYU Special Collections Librarian.

The inscription of the gravestone at Buckton-Union Cemetery Stockholm, New York has been copied: "Asahel Smith. d. Nov. 1, 1830. age 87 yrs." Lindon E. Riggs, "St. Lawrence Co., N. Y., Cemetery Records" [n.p., n.d.]. George A. Smith's note in the family Bible gives the date of death one day earlier.

[218]John Smith, Journal, Jan. 26, 1833.

[219]Letter of Hyrum Smith to Elias Smith, Feb. 27, 1836, Kirtland, Ohio, typescript copy, LDS Historian's Office.

[220]Eliza R. Snow's recollections, reporting the words of "a messenger": "I was present, on the 17th of May, when a messenger arrived and informed the Prophet Joseph that his grandmother, Mary Duty Smith, had arrived at Fairport, on her way to Kirtland, and wished him to come for her. The messenger stated that she said she had asked the Lord that she might live to see her children and grandchildren once more." Edward W. Tullidge, *Women of Mormondon* (New York, 1877), p. 97. If Eliza Snow is correct on the date, the Prophet already knew of his grandmother's arrival—it is possible that Eliza Snow was present when Joseph's cousin

Elias Smith was talking about their grandmother, since his journal reports staying at Kirtland with Hyrum May 16, then going with Hyrum and Joseph the next day for their grandmother.

Final descriptions of Mary Duty Smith vary slightly on her age. Her birthdate in town records in Oct. 11, 1743 (n. 127).

[221]Edward W. Tullidge, "Judge Smith," *History of Salt Lake City and Its Founders* (Salt Lake City, 1886), p. 157. Elias Smith was 80 at the publication of the Tullidge biography and lived four years longer. Tullidge no doubt interviewed Elias Smith, since he gives minute details that go beyond but agree with Smith's journal, which (for May 16, 1836) reads, "landed at Fairport, Geauga County, Ohio, twelve miles from Kirtland, about 5 p.m. Here I met Joseph and Hyrum Smith, and having grandmother and the brethren at Fairport, proceeded in the rain, though it had been fair till after we landed, to Kirtland with Joseph and Hyrum, when we arrived at 11 o'clock at night. Stayed with Hyrum Smith." George A. Smith was the descendant who did not see his grandmother, since he was away on a mission at her return. Like his cousin Elias, he notes this fact in his memoirs: "She saw all the grandchildren and great-grandchildren that were in Ohio, except myself."

[222]Elias Smith, Journal, May 17, 1836.

[223]Lucy Smith, *Biographical Sketches,* p. 213. The quotation's concluding phrase, "whom she expected never to see," possibly refers to the preceding word, "great-grandchildren," since Mary expected to see her children and grandchildren but would have been impressed by many additional descendants that she met.

[224]Snow recollections, cit. Tullidge, *Women of Mormondom*, p. 98. The first bracket of the quotation [Jr.] is mine, but the second phrase [the patriarch] appears in Eliza Snow's recollection in parentheses, though it is here bracketed as probably not part of the original expression of Mary Smith.

Cp. the autobiography of Jesse N. Smith, son of Asael, Jr., who was but a child at the migration to Kirtland, though had access to family information: "My grandmother Smith accompanied us to Kirtland. . . . She had expressed a desire to be baptized, but being infirm it was not done."

Cp. the notebook copying first-person journal entries from the Smith family, the following comments from a daughter-in-law living near Asael and Mary Duty Smith in New York, perhaps John's wife: "He [Asael Smith, Sr.] left his wife, also a firm believer, and she would have been baptized, but Jesse, her oldest son, was so opposed that she concluded to delay the matter until she could get to Kirtland. When she arrived there she said to Lucy, 'I am going to have your Joseph baptize me, but I will have my blessing from my Joseph.' But in 20 days after she got there she was taken sick and died in the 93 year of her age, surrounded with a numerous company of children, grandchildren, and great-grandchildren." "Copy of an Old Notebook" (cit. n. 217), pp. 41-42, called to my attention through the friendship of Buddy Youngreen.

[225]Tullidge, *Women of Mormondom*, pp. 97-98. Elias Smith's journal suggests that his father, who was remembered at this gathering, arrived May 19.

[226]Eliza Snow recalled: "I was present, on the 17th of May, when a messenger arrived and informed the Prophet Joseph that his grandmother, Mary Duty Smith, had arrived at Fairport, on her way to Kirtland, and wished him to come for her. . . . The Prophet responded with earnestness, 'I wish she had set the time longer.' I pondered in silence over this remark, thinking there might be more meaning in the expression than the words indicated, which was proven by the result, for she only lived a few days after her arrival." Tullidge, *Women of Mormondom*, p. 97.

[227]Ibid., pp. 98-99. The account in Joseph Smith, *History of the Church*, vol. 2, pp. 441-42, is apparently of later origin than Kirtland; it has not been utilized here, except for the date of death. It adds the fact of interment "in the burial ground near the temple, after a funeral address had been delivered by Sidney Rigdon."

[228]Speech of George A. Smith, July 7, 1872, *Journal of Discourses*, vol. 15 (Liverpool, 1873), p. 98, the same talk in which he mentions his grandfather's notice of his interest in family background (p. 97).

[229]Journal of John Smith, cit. Lucy Smith, *Biographical Sketches*, p. 155.

[230]George A. Smith, "Memoirs," Jan. 9, 1832.

[231]*Deseret News*, May 25, 1854. Brackets correct erroneous information, such as the 1833 date for conversion. John Smith's highest administrative appointment is not mentioned, "assistant counselor" to Joseph Smith in the First Presidency in 1837. Joseph Smith, *History*, vol. 2, p. 509. Three times John Smith was sustained as a

stake president: Adam-ondi-Ahman, Nauvoo, and Salt Lake Valley localities.

[232]Henry Follansbee Long, "The Salt Marshes of the Massachusetts Coast," *Historical Collections of . . . Topsfield,* vol. 15 (1910), pp. 119-20.

[233]All deletions are indicated, with exception of minor dittographies and occasional substitution of "were" for "was," indicated by brackets. For readability, abbreviations have been spelled out, spelling errors corrected, and present-day forms printed, since few archaic usages exist. Capitalization and punctuation are imposed by present standards. The spelling "Asael" is also regularized, since John's account varies between this spelling and also "Asahel." Cp. n. 169.

[234]A brief introduction dated "GSL City, April 5, 1851" heads the document from which the quoted phrases are taken. Dictation is apparent by reference to writing "by the hand of John," his son. This account appears in a ledger-size book apparently intended for family history, as distinct from the smaller journal in which John Smith first made his family record in 1839.

[235]"Son Ahman" is a term early used by Joseph Smith for the Savior, as shown in Doctrine and Covenants 78:20 and 95:17, revelations of 1832 and 1833. Orson Pratt recalled its basic meaning as simply "Son of God." *Journal of Discourses,* vol. 2 (Liverpool, 1855), p. 342 (Feb. 18, 1855, discourse).

[236]For documentary evidence on the migration and life of Robert Smith, see Archibald F. Bennett, "The Ancestry of Joseph Smith the Prophet," *Utah Genealogical and Historical Magazine,* vol. 20, (1929), pp. 16-17.

[237]For birthdates see n. 193.

[238]The 1851 version adds: "My grandfather was [a] businessman, was a justice under the British government before the Revolution and was a member of British Parliament [Massachusetts colonial legislature] for years. When the Revolution broke out, he fought under Washington." It has not been determined that Asael's father, Samuel Smith, served military duty in the Revolution—service of Samuel Smith of Topsfield might refer to Asael's brother, not necessarily his father. See *Massachusetts Soldiers and Sailors in the Revolutionary War* (Boston, 1907), vol. 15, p. 537.

[239]The 1851 version clarifies this sentence as spoken by Asael's father: "The old man said, 'Asael says he will take care of my wife.'"

[240]The 1851 version adds: "I have often heard him say he had paid $60 for a mug of flip." This comment supports the obvious conclusion that John Smith's history often repeats what his father Asael had told John about his life.

[241]John Smith's spelling corresponds to the marriage record of Priscilla Gould's nephew Daniel Bixby, the more usual spelling in local records. Though the marriage in 1776 is recorded as "Bigsbee," his birth (1751) and death (1825) are recorded as "Bixby." *Vital Records of Topsfield,* pp. 16, 122, 206. In her will of May 15, 1794, Priscilla Smith named her sister "Ruth Bixby, widow of Daniel Bixby, Jr." Probate Records, Essex Co., Salem, Mass., File 25718. Since the couple had but one son, the only Bixby who was a nephew of Priscilla would be the Daniel whose vital dates are given above. He is identified in Gould, *Family of Zaccheus Gould,* pp. 54, 67.

[242]The final clause of the 1851 version reads: "where it could be loaded on a wagon."

[243]The summary of migration was reworded in 1851: "It was a new country, and the roads were very bad. And we got along very slow, being very heavy loaded. We were about 14 days passing through New Hampshire, my native state."

[244]Francis Parkman, *Montcalm and Wolfe* (reprint; New York, 1962), p. 429.

[245]Martin B. Duberman, *Charles Francis Adams* (Boston, 1961), p. 2.

[246]Joseph Smith, discourse of May 21, 1843, Joseph Smith, *History,* vol. 5, p. 401.

[247]Mack, *Narrative,* pp. 15, 20-21. Solomon's conduct never exceeded the one revelry mentioned: "such a day I never saw before nor since" (p. 15).

[248]Putnam, "Danvers, at Home and Abroad," No. 60. On Putnam, see n. 156.

[249]Richard Lloyd Anderson, "The Smiths Who Handled the Plates," *Improvement Era,* vol. 72 (1969), pp. 28-34.

[250]Interview with William Smith, *Zion's Ensign,* vol. 5 (1894), No. 3, p. 6. See Richard Lloyd Anderson, "The Trustworthiness of Young Joseph Smith," *Improvement Era,* vol. 73 (1970), pp. 82-89.

Notes on Illustrations

Illustration Page	*Credits and Background*
	Solomon Mack, Jr., and both were baptized into the church founded by their cousin, Joseph Smith, Jr. (ibid., p. 124).
71	Photograph of drawing by John Warner Barber, *Historical Collections . . . of Every Town in Massachusetts* (Worcester, 1840), the preface of which indicates completion of all work in Apr. 1839.
90	This map locates villages or civic centers, generally only approximate for residences in the larger area covered by the eastern township.
93	Photograph from George Francis Dow, *History of Topsfield, Massachusetts* (Topsfield, 1940). The church on the left is built on the site of that in which Asael Smith had his children baptized and held a pew.
96	The photograph was originally printed by John H. Towne, "Topsfield Houses and Buildings," *Historical Collections of the Topsfield Historical Society,* vol. 8 (1902), between pages 44-45, which sketched the history of the home. The photograph was republished with short discussion in the *Collections,* vol. 29 (1928), pp. 87-88, by Sidney Perley, "Topsfield Houses and Lands." Cp. George Francis Dow, *History of Topsfield, Massachusetts* (Topsfield, 1940), p. 355. Towne, a capable historian, was sure that this house was built in 1690. The property was purchased by Asael Smith's father in 1764 (n. 123); shortly after Asael sold it, it was described as follows: "house; 800 sq. ft.; 2 stories; 9 windows; 31 sq. ft. glass; value $120." Harriet S. Tapley (ed.), "The United States Direct Tax of 1798, as Assessed on Topsfield," *Historical Collections of the Topsfield Historical Society,* vol. 7 (1901), p. 60. Of the works cited above, Perley seems to have specific knowledge that the house was demolished in 1876, which is harmonious with the 1885 information that the dwelling "was torn down nine or ten years ago" (n. 123 herein).

Illustration Page	Credits and Background
103	Photograph by George Edward Anderson, about 1908, by permission of LDS Historian's Office.
121-23	See beginning of chapter 6.
130-40	See beginning of chapter 6.
142	Early photographs held by the LDS Historian's Office, published with permission.
146	Photograph from Currier, *History of Newbury,* republished by Henry Follansbee Long, "The Salt Marshes of the Massachusetts Coast," *Historical Collections of the Topsfield Historical Society,* vol. 15 (1910), facing p. 105. It is captioned "The Marshes at Newbury," the town immediately north of Ipswich.

Reference Bibliography

Book lists have different purposes, and this one simply identifies works cited by short title in the footnotes. Pertinent sources on the Prophet's New England ancestors can be obtained by studying the footnotes, which relate a given document to a particular problem, as in the case of church or public records (town minutes, deeds, probate proceedings, vital dates, and assessments). Most of these materials have not been listed in the bibliography because they are either in the locality named or on microfilm in a major genealogical library, as that of the LDS Genealogical Society in Salt Lake City. Nor are standard collections included here separately, such as the *Journal of Discourses* or the *Historical Collections of the Topsfield Historical Society*, the latter title shortened in citations. If a book or manuscript has a footnote reference in short form, it will be found on the following list. No reference appears here if it is used only once, or if publication information could be conveniently repeated or referred to in the footnote section. The result is a summary of non-public sources most used in recreating the lives of Joseph Smith's grandparents.

Anderson, Mary Audentia Smith. *Ancestry and Posterity of Joseph Smith and Emma Hale.* Independence, Mo., 1929.

Bennett, Archibald F. "Solomon Mack and His Family." *Improvement Era,* vol. 58 (1955) and vol. 59 (1956). This series ran from September 1955 through May 1956.

Connecticut Vital Records Index. LDS Genealogical Society copy of the Lucius Barnes Barbour card index at the Connecticut State Library, Hartford.

Dow, George Francis. *History of Topsfield, Massachusetts.* Topsfield, 1940.

Fergusson, Charles Bruce, ed. *Diary of Simeon Perkins, 1797-1803.* *Publications of the Champlain Society,* vol. 43. Toronto, 1967.

Gould, Benjamin Apthorp. *The Family of Zaccheus Gould of Topsfield.* Lynn, Mass., 1895.

Harvey, D. C., and Fergusson, C. Bruce, eds. *Diary of Simeon Perkins, 1780-1789.* *Publications of the Champlain Society,* vol. 36. Toronto, 1958.

Hayward, Silvanus. *History of the Town of Gilsum, New Hampshire.* Manchester, N. H., 1881.

Lovejoy, Evelyn M. Wood. *History of Royalton, Vermont.* Burlington, Vt., 1911.

Mack, Solomon. *A Narrative of the Life of Solomon Mack.* Windsor, Vt., [1811]. Complete historical portions of this work are reprinted herein as chapter 3. For the date of publication, see n. 3.

Martin, Sophia. *Mack Genealogy: The Descendants of John Mack of Lyme, Conn.* Rutland, Vt., 1903.

"Narrative of the Life of Joseph Tuttle." Two typescript copies are known: one held by a descendant in Painesville, Ohio, a copy of which is at the Morley Public Library in Painesville, and the other in possession of the Mahoning Valley Historical Society, Youngstown, Ohio. Background appears in n. 50.

Putnam, Rev. Alfred Porter. "Danvers, at Home and Abroad," No. 60. *Danvers* [Mass.] *Mirror,* September 19, 1885. Background appears in n. 156.

Smith, Asael. Address to His Family, April 10, 1799. The entire document is printed in photographic facsimile and also transcription herein, chapter 6.

_____. Letter to Jacob Towne, January 14, 1796. The entire document is printed in photographic facsimile and also transcription herein, chapter 6, by permission of the repository, Essex Institute, Salem, Mass.

Smith, John. Journal. The entire entry of July 20, 1839, is reprinted herein as chapter 7, with background information.

Smith, George A. Correspondence with Humphrey Gould, various dates. Originals are held in the Beinecke Library at Yale University, which has authorized their use herein.

_____. "Memoirs," the written title of his manuscript autobiography. Sections cited on family history are in the beginning pages.

Smith, Joseph. *History of the Church of Jesus Christ of Latter-day Saints.* Salt Lake City, 1902, the publication date of the first volume. Subsequent volumes have different printing and reissue dates, but pagination in these is the same.

Smith, Joseph F., Jr. (President Joseph Fielding Smith). "Asahel Smith of Topsfield, with Some Account of the Smith Family." *Historical Collections of the Topsfield Historical Society,* vol. 8 (1902), pp., 87-101.

Smith, Lucy. *Biographical Sketches of Joseph Smith.* Liverpool, 1853. For information on editions, see the Source Note herein, p. xv.

Tullidge, Edward. *Women of Mormondom.* New York, 1877.

Vital Records of Montague, Massachusetts, to the End of the Year 1849. Salem, Mass., 1934.

Vital Records of Topsfield, Massachusetts, to the End of the Year 1849. Topsfield, Mass., 1903.

Index

Additional unindexed information is in Notes on Text. Notes 81-86, 127, 193-208 are especially helpful on the wives and families of Asael Smith and Solomon Mack.

Smith, Lucy Mack: birth, 18; character, 28-29; marriage, 64; 107;
  personality revealed in writing, 63-64.
Smith, Mary, 170, 140.
Smith, Mary Duty: character, 168-69; death, 115; migration to
  Kirtland, 114-15; religious convictions, 115.
Smith, Priscilla, 170, 140.
Smith, Samuel, son of Asael Sr., 140.
Smith, Samuel, father of Asael Sr., death, 94-95; prominence, 90-91;
  , 140.
Smith, Silas, 109, 140.
Smith, Stephen, 110, 140.
Smith, Susan, 140.
Tuttle, Lovisa, see Mack, Lovisa.

*Additional numbered information is in Notes on Text. Notes 51-52,
112, 192-204 are especially helpful on the wives and families of
Asael Smith and Solomon Mack.*

DATE DUE

NOV 16 '76
FEB 22 '78
MAR 20 '78
APR 18 '78
NOV 27 '79
DEC 3 '80
AN 2 1 1981.
JUL 18 '88

DEMCO 38-297

Lincoln Christian College

J